**W9-BDW-351**

THE DEATH PENALTY

What's Keeping It Alive

Andrea D. Lyon

ROWMAN & LITTLEFIELD
Lanham • Boulder • New York • London

Published by Rowman & Littlefield
A wholly owned subsidiary of
The Rowman & Littlefield Publishing Group, Inc.
4501 Forbes Boulevard, Suite 200, Lanham, Maryland 20706
www.rowman.com

Unit A, Whitacre Mews, 26-34 Stannery Street, London SE11 4AB,
United Kingdom

British Library Cataloguing in Publication Information Available

Library of Congress Cataloging-in-Publication Data
Lyon, Andrea D.
The death penalty : what's keeping it alive / Andrea D. Lyon.
pages cm
Includes bibliographical references and index.
ISBN 978-1-4422-3267-9 (cloth : alk. paper) — ISBN 978-1-4422-3268-
6 (electronic)
1. Capital punishment—United States—History. I. Title.
HV8699.U5L96 2015
364.660973—dc23
2014025513

∞ ™ The paper used in this publication meets the minimum requirements of American National Standard for Information Sciences Perma-
nence of Paper for Printed Library Materials, ANSI/NISO Z39.48-1992.

Printed in the United States of America

For my father

CONTENTS

PREFACE

While most people have seen trials on television, fictional or otherwise, most have not been in courtrooms themselves. In a criminal trial, there is usually an obvious divide between the courtroom observers—what I jokingly call the bride's side and the groom's side. The bride's side is the defense (in my mind at least), and the groom's side is the prosecution. That is, the prosecution team sits on the side of the courtroom closest to the jury and their supporters do, too. The defense sits at the other table and the defendant's family or supporters sit on that side.

Nowhere is this divide more apparent than in a death penalty trial. Emotions run high, and at the point a jury is considering whether to execute the defendant, they can rise to a fever pitch.

When I was a member of the Chicago Public Defender's Homicide Task Force, there were times when we represented people whom no one cared to support in any way. They were often charged with awful crimes, facing the death penalty, and their families had long since given up on them. One such case was that of a man named Edgar Hope. Hope was charged with the killing of an Irish police officer on a bus. There had been a disturbance on the bus and the driver had called the police. The officer came on the bus, located Hope and searched him, but missed the gun Hope had on him. A struggle ensued and Hope shot the officer in front of many passengers.

The only issue in the case was the punishment. There was no question of guilt. There was no question that he was eligible to be sentenced to death under the Illinois statute for the killing of a police officer in the line of duty. The only question was whether the jury would sentence him to death or to life in prison.

This particular defendant didn't have any family, and so some of us—that is, other public defenders—would come to court and sit on that side of the courtroom in support of our beleaguered colleagues.

The trial resulted in conviction, a foregone conclusion. The jury took no time to find him eligible for death (not every murder can be a death case—the prosecution has to show first-degree murder plus an aggravating or eligibility factor). The word went out in the criminal courts building that there was a verdict on the death penalty hearing. We all knew what it would be. An Irish judge had presided over an all-white jury that had been exhorted by two white prosecutors. It was an election year. There was a dead police officer.

I went to the courtroom to lend support to my public defender colleagues. I looked across the aisle to the prosecution's side. There were rows of prosecutors there; perhaps thirty or so. All of them were lawyers. They had all gone to college, as I had, and done reasonably well. They had all gone to law school, as I had, and done reasonably well there, too. They had all passed the Illinois bar exam, too, as had I, and had sworn to uphold the laws of the United States and Illinois, as I had. More than that, as prosecutors, they promised to represent the people of the state of Illinois, which included me, the defendant on trial, and everyone else in that courtroom.

When the defendant was brought out from the lock-up, everyone stood as the verdict—in this case what the sentence was to be—was read. It was death.

When it was read, those prosecutors stood and cheered. And they yelled, "Kill him! Kill him! Kill him!"

That is when I realized, beyond any doubt, that the death penalty was both more and less than the "ultimate punishment" for murder.

This book draws on my years as a death penalty defender as well as extensive research on the subject to analyze why the death penalty remains such a fixture of the justice system, in spite of its many documented flaws, such as wrongful convictions, racial and socioeconomic bias, and problems with executions themselves, most recently the botched execution in Oklahoma of Clayton Lockett. On April 29, 2014, Lockett died of a heart attack approximately 40 minutes after the state began administering a new lethal injection protocol. Lockett received an injection of midazolam, the first drug in a three-drug protocol, at 6:23 p.m. At 6:33, Lockett was declared unconscious, but about three minutes later, witnesses said he began to nod, mumble, and writhe on the gurney. Some witnesses described his movements as a seizure. At 7:06, Lockett died of a massive heart attack. Jerry Massie, a spokesman for the Oklahoma Department of Corrections, said, "The director did say that it appears that a vein blew up or exploded, it collapsed, and the drugs were not getting into the system like they were supposed to."[1] Many found this deeply disturbing, including the President of the United States, and as professor Austin Sarat has said in his new book *Gruesome Spectacles: Botched Executions and America's Death Penalty*, which describes the history of flawed executions in the United States from 1890 to 2010, "[w]ith each development in the technology of execution, the same promises have been made, that each new technology was safe, reliable, effective and humane. Those claims have not generally been fulfilled."[2]

We spend more to execute than to incarcerate, there is no evidence that the death penalty deters violent crime, we convict and sentence the innocent, and, as can be seen, we brutalize all of us in the process.

This book explores the nature of the death penalty as a political statement and tool in order to try to answer the question posed by the book's title: what's keeping the death penalty alive?

ACKNOWLEDGMENTS

I want to thank my steadfast editors, Joan Liebsen-Smith, Mary Bandstra, and Melissa Hernandez. I also want to thank University of Iowa law students Zane Ulmstead and Ryan Beckenbaugh, and DePaul University College of Law students Melissa Hernandez and Alana de Leon for their assistance in both research and writing.

I also want to thank the many teachers I have had, both in school and out, who taught me to look beneath the surface, to solve problems vertically, and to care about the world and its inhabitants.

I

THE DEATH PENALTY YESTERDAY AND TODAY

On January 17, 1977, Gary Gilmore was executed by a firing squad in the state of Utah. The night before, his relatives visited with him for the last time. His uncle snuck in some whiskey for Gilmore to drink. Gilmore's attorney notified Johnny Cash that he was Gilmore's favorite singer, and Cash called the prison to sing him a song. Gilmore sang along.

The next morning, at 8:00 a.m., the firing squad assembled. Five volunteers placed the barrels of their rifles through holes in a wall. Each rifle aimed at Gilmore—strapped to a chair with a paper target placed over his heart and a black hood placed over his head. A wall of sandbags stood behind Gilmore to catch the bullets that aimed in his direction. At 8:07 a.m. the squad members pulled their respective triggers, and Gary Gilmore was executed. His last words were, "Let's do it."

In October 1976, Gilmore had been convicted for the murder of a motel manager in Provo, Utah, and sentenced to death. Although defendants sentenced to the death penalty generally choose to challenge their sentences, favoring the alternative of life imprisonment to the prospect of execution, Gilmore accepted his death sentence without protest. Nevertheless, many anti–death penalty groups acted in what they saw as Gilmore's best interest and fought against his execution. The American Civil Liberties Union (ACLU) and the National Association for the Advancement of Colored People (NAACP) got involved. Even Gilmore's mother and brother sought to stay his execution, until Gilmore finally convinced them of his wishes to see his sentence through.

As Gilmore said during the sentencing review hearing in front of the Board of Pardons (which was orchestrated by Utah's governor, against Gilmore's wishes), "I took them literal and serious when they sentenced me to death. I thought you were supposed to take them serious. I didn't know it was a joke. I would like them all . . . to just butt out. This is my life and this is my death. It's been sanctioned by the courts that I die and I accept that."[1]

But death penalty opponents were not as accepting as Gilmore was, and they did not "butt out." The ACLU, in particular, continued to fight the execution. While Gilmore was celebrating his last night with his friends, his family, and Johnny Cash, the ACLU secured a last-minute stay of execution from a federal judge in Salt Lake City. However, the stay was quickly overturned by the Tenth Circuit Court of Appeals. Gilmore's death went forward as planned.

Gary Gilmore was not only notable for his unusual acceptance of the death sentence issued against him, he was also the first person executed in the United States following the United States Supreme Court's 1972 decision in *Furman v. Georgia*, which had effectively nullified all then-existing death penalty statutes as unconstitutional due to their inconsistent and arbitrary application.[2] For example, the same crime committed in two different counties would result in one defendant being executed and the other receiving a term of years, there were documented racial disparities, and indeed the United States Supreme Court called the application of the death penalty so arbitrary as to be akin to being struck by lightning. The decision led to a nationwide freeze on executions. State legislatures spent the ensuing years after *Furman* rewriting their death penalty statutes to eliminate the arbitrary application that the Supreme Court had found unconstitutional, and in 1976, in *Gregg v. Georgia*, the Court affirmed that the death penalty itself was constitutional, provided that it is applied objectively.[3] After the short-lived pause in executions, the death penalty was back. It was within this turbulent context that the ACLU and NAACP fought to keep Gary Gilmore's execution at bay. Despite their efforts, Gilmore became the new death penalty's first victim.

✳ ✳ ✳

The death penalty dates back to early human civilization. It was first established by law in the eighteenth century B.C., in the Code of King Hammurabi of Babylon, which contained twenty-five crimes that were punishable by death. In the seventh century B.C., Athens' Draconian Code prescribed death for all crimes, eliminating any punishment distinction between more- or less-reprehensible crimes.[4] And, of course, Jesus of Nazareth was sentenced to death by Pontius Pilate and was crucified for the charged crime of blasphemy.[5]

By the time European colonists settled in America, the death penalty was firmly established in their home countries. As such, they brought the tradition of capital punishment to American shores. In April 1607, one hundred and four settlers arrived in America to establish the first permanent English settlement in Jamestown, Virginia. Only thirty-eight of the settlers survived the first harsh winter.[6] One of those few survivors, Captain George Kendall, was executed in 1608 for acting as a Spanish spy. As the American colonies began to take shape, executions became commonplace for even petty crimes, with new criminal statutes in the various colonies authorizing death for such offenses as stealing grapes, killing chickens, and trading with the natives.[7]

Yet, like the American settlers who were influenced by European views of the death penalty when they established the American colonies, the settlers' views largely continued to mirror those of their European counterparts through the commencement of the Revolutionary War. As European philosophers like Montesquieu, Voltaire, Jeremy Bentham, and particularly Cesare Beccaria wrote against government-sponsored executions, their viewpoints influenced reformers in both Europe and in the American colonies. Thomas Jefferson was one such reformer, and he relied upon Beccaria's essay, *On Crimes and Punishment*, to garner support for a bill intended to revise Virginia's death penalty laws. Jefferson's bill would have dramatically reduced the number of crimes eligible for the death penalty, down to only murder and treason, but it failed to pass by a single vote.

Other early reformers found more success than Jefferson, however. In Pennsylvania, Dr. Benjamin Rush founded the Pennsylvania Prison Society and, with the support of Benjamin Franklin, he led Pennsylvania to be the first state to draw distinctions between degrees of murder. Then, in 1794, Rush was instrumental in reducing Pennsylvania's application of the death penalty to only first-degree murder, the highest level of murder.

Pennsylvania remained at the forefront of the death penalty abolition movement throughout the nineteenth century. In the early years of that century, the other northeastern states followed Pennsylvania's lead by dramatically reducing the number of capital crimes, ensuring that citizens would no longer face a death sentence for any but the most egregious of crimes.

Besides reducing the number of crimes warranting the death penalty, Pennsylvania and its neighbors also radically changed how executions were carried out. The European and earliest American traditions treated executions as public spectacles, and those who were condemned to die were executed in the town square for all the local citizens to see. The nineteenth century saw a radical transformation.[8] In 1834, Pennsylvania became the first state to eliminate public "ceremonial" executions by removing them to correctional facilities, away from the eye of casual observers. There were a number of reasons why this occurred, not the least of which was that the occasion of public executions often caused unlawful and riotous behavior among the observers. Other states soon followed.

As the nineteenth century phased into the twentieth century, the death penalty abolition movement waxed and waned. In the years leading up to World War I, nine states had completely outlawed the death penalty; however, five of those nine reinstated it shortly after the war.[9] The decades following World War I saw more executions than any other era in United States history. Coinciding with Prohibition and the Great Depression, criminologists during the 1920s and 1930s advocated for the death penalty as protection against social and moral decay. These views were fundamentally at odds with the eighteenth-century philosophers who had staunchly refuted similar claims, but the new attitudes on the death penalty manifested themselves in dramatic fashion: in the 1930s, there were an average of 167 executions per year, more than in any other decade in American history.[10] And as science and technology advanced during this era, the methods of execution "advanced" in response: New York introduced the electric chair in 1890, and Nevada introduced the gas chamber in 1924. Both methods stemmed from a desire for "more humane" executions, which were intended to lead sentencing judges and juries in the 1930s to feel more comfortable with issuing death sentences to more people than ever before.

Although the post–World War I period saw a dramatic increase in America's application of the death penalty, World War II had the opposite effect. Framed against the backdrop of the atrocities that Nazi Germany inflicted on European Jews and others, which had resulted in the systematic killing of more than six million people, Americans grew understandably critical of death penalty regimes that permitted their own government to kill its own citizens. Perhaps as a result of the Holocaust connotations, the number of executions dropped sharply from the 1940s through the 1970s.

The executions that did occur during this time period, however, revealed a troubling trend: African Americans comprised a disproportionate share of those executed. The Civil Rights movement took note of this trend and, along with other social justice advocates who emerged during the Vietnam War era, began to use the courts to challenge the constitutional validity of the death penalty.

✻ ✻ ✻

The Eighth Amendment of the United States Constitution states: "Excessive bail shall not be required, nor excessive

fines imposed, nor cruel and unusual punishments inflicted."
As death penalty opponents sought to challenge the validity
of capital punishment, they premised their argument on the
"cruel and unusual punishments" clause. The Supreme
Court provided a framework for legal challenges to the death
penalty in 1958, in *Trop v. Dulles*, when it stated that the
Eighth Amendment contemplated an "evolving standard of
decency that marked the progress of a maturing society."[11]
Because it is an "evolving standard," the mere fact that the
drafters of the Constitution did not find the death penalty
cruel and unusual when they wrote the amendment does not
preclude the Supreme Court from finding it cruel and unusual in contemporary society.

Initial attacks on the death penalty dealt with how death
sentences were issued. In *United States v. Jackson*, the Supreme Court decided that criminal statutes permitting the
death penalty may not give the death-sentencing power sole-
ly to the jury. The Court reasoned that giving juries the sole
power to impose a death sentence improperly coerced defendants to plead guilty and forgo a jury trial for fear of
execution.[12] Another case, also decided in 1968, *Witherspoon v. Illinois*, clarified the jury selection process for trials
implicating the death penalty. In *Witherspoon* the Court
held that jurors with "religious or conscientious" scruples
against the death penalty may nevertheless sit on a capital
jury, so long as the juror adequately assures the court that he
or she can make an impartial decision regarding punishment.[13]

It was not until 1972's *Furman v. Georgia* that the Court addressed the substantive question of whether death penalty statutes comported with the Eighth Amendment's protections against cruel and unusual punishment. In *Furman*, a series of defendants who had been sentenced to death appealed their sentences on the grounds that the jury's broad discretion in deciding whether they lived or died resulted in the arbitrary imposition of the death sentence. All of the *Furman* defendants were convicted and sentenced by the same jury during the same deliberations, and each defendant was African American. The Court observed that under the existing model of broad jury discretion, "the death penalty [was] exacted with great infrequency even for the most atrocious crimes and that there is no meaningful basis for distinguishing the few cases in which it is imposed from the many cases in which it is not."[14] The Court also noted that the unpredictable application of the death penalty was "an open invitation to discrimination."[15]

Despite strong outright disapproval of the death penalty expressed by some of the justices,[16] the Court's decision in *Furman* was only 5–4 and its ultimate impact was relatively narrow. Rather than categorically eliminating the death penalty as unconstitutional under the Eighth Amendment, the Court held only that the existing one-jury, one-deliberation system for issuing the death penalty violated the Eighth Amendment. Although *Furman* brought the death penalty to a temporary halt by voiding nearly every death penalty statute as it currently existed, state and federal legislatures convened to rewrite their statutes to comport with the *Furman* decision's constitutional mandates.

In 1976, the Court began assessing the newly revised death penalty statutes that appeared after *Furman*. North Carolina addressed the excessive jury discretion concerns by eliminating sentencing discretion altogether and mandating the death penalty for all defendants convicted of capital crimes. However, the Supreme Court held this practice unconstitutional in 1976's *Woodson v. North Carolina*.[17] Other states adopted a more nuanced approach.

In *Gregg v. Georgia*, the Court reviewed a death penalty scheme—introduced in Georgia, Texas, and Florida—that created a two-part system for finding guilt and sentencing death, referred to as bifurcated proceedings by the courts. A death penalty case is really two trials. First, it's a trial on the merits: Did the defendant commit the crime? If he did, was it first-degree murder? In some jurisdictions, the question of eligibility for the death penalty is answered at the trial on the merits. This means that in order for the prosecution to even ask for the death penalty, it must prove a first-degree murder as well as an aggravating factor that takes the case into the (allegedly) small group of cases where the death penalty can even be sought. A common aggravating factor that makes a first-degree murder case into a capital case is the first-degree murder of a police officer acting in the line of duty, or a first-degree murder during a rape.

Assuming the prosecution is able to establish both guilt and eligibility beyond a reasonable doubt, the jury then de-

THE DEATH PENALTY YESTERDAY AND TODAY

cides whether death is the appropriate choice of punishment. At that part of the trial, the prosecution may present aggravating evidence, some of which is statutory and some of which is not. Some examples might include prior criminal record or other violent acts that were not charged or that did not result in a conviction and victim impact evidence. Mitigation—reasons to punish with imprisonment rather than death—is any evidence that might tend to explain the client's actions, family history, mental health issues, physical health matters, or the impact the client's execution would have on his or her loved ones. The rules of evidence are relaxed at a penalty phase; in most states, this means that anything that is "relevant and reliable" is admissible.[18] Generally speaking, evidence cannot be introduced at trial if it does not adhere to certain rules—for example, an out-of-court statement is considered hearsay and can only be admitted under limited circumstances at a trial. At a penalty phase hearing, however, hearsay is nearly always admissible.

Before arriving at the issue of whether the bifurcated death penalty statutes were constitutional, the Court first explicitly clarified that its *Furman* holding did not find the death penalty to be categorically unconstitutional, only that it required sufficient procedures to objectively guide its application. And the Court ultimately concluded that the bifurcated model, accompanied by judge-issued instructions regarding the weight that the jury must give to the relevant factors, was a constitutionally adequate system for objectively issuing death sentences.[19]

With the *Gregg* opinion providing necessary guidance to state and federal lawmakers regarding constitutionally permissible death sentencing procedure, the moratorium on executions that had begun in *Furman* was officially over. After a brief period of uncertainty, the waters were cleared: the death penalty was not per se unconstitutional. States could once again execute their death row inmates. Just six months after *Gregg* lifted the moratorium, Gary Gilmore was the first person to be executed under the revised American death penalty.

✣ ✣ ✣

With capital sentencing procedure settled, the post-*Gregg* death penalty regime looks different than the pre-*Gregg* regime. Today, jurisdictions have generally adopted the bifurcated approach upheld in *Gregg*, but some states have tweaked which entity has the final power to sentence a defendant to death. For example, certain states (Arizona, Idaho, Montana, and Nebraska) allow the judge—not the jury—to make the final decision on a death sentence; other states (Alabama, Delaware, and Florida)[20] grant juries the power to recommend a death sentence, but permit the presiding judge to override the recommendation.[21]

Jurisdictions have likewise created elaborate systems of post-sentencing appellate review. In noncapital cases, defendants must choose whether or not to appeal and must go through an intermediate appellate court before receiving a nonguaranteed secondary appeal to the highest-level court. In capital cases, however, any death sentence imposed by the judge or jury is automatically appealed to the highest-level court, which must evaluate the trial for errors and may determine whether death is a proportional punishment for the crime. This appellate structure, like the bifurcated system, was addressed and upheld in *Gregg v. Georgia*.

Even when the automatic direct appeal is unsuccessful, a convicted defendant can engage in a federal habeas corpus petition, widely referred to as a "collateral attack" on the initially imposed sentence. Because habeas corpus petitions operate in federal courts, they must allege a violation of the United States Constitution, and not a violation of state law or a state constitution. Habeas petitions are reviewed first in a United States District Court, then move to the Circuit Courts, and potentially to the Supreme Court. This route for constitutional review presents a second level of potential relief for a capital-convicted defendant, but unlike the automatic review given by state courts, federal habeas corpus relief is not mandatory. In order to receive consideration for habeas corpus, the onus is on defendants to proactively formulate their petitions and submit them for review. What follows is a chart to look at the various stages of a capital case.

The state and federal opportunities to appeal a death sentence provide convicted defendants subjected to the harshest of criminal penalties unique access to review of their sentences. In the approximately twenty years following

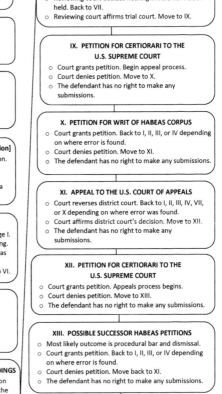

Figure 1.1.   Stages of a Death Penalty Case

Gregg's reinstitution of the death penalty, empirical studies have shown that these appellate procedures had a significant impact on affording relief to defendants sentenced to the death penalty. For instance, regarding the success rate of automatic state-review proceedings: "[o]f the 5,760 death sentences imposed in the [period between 1973 and 1995], 4,578 (78%) were finally reviewed on 'direct appeal' by a state high court. Of those, 1,885 (41%) were thrown out on the basis of 'serious error.'"[22] Likewise, of the death sentences challenged in federal habeas corpus petitions after surviving state review, 40 percent were overturned due to serious error.[23] In combination, then, the total percentage of death sentences overturned through state and federal review amounted to 68 percent between 1973 and 1995.[24]

The data revealing defendants' success in overturning their death sentences is certainly laudable for the individual defendants' ability to avoid execution and receive commutations to life imprisonment, but it conversely raises the concern that the death penalty system, constitutionally optimized in *Gregg*, erroneously sentences defendants to death at a 68 percent clip. That these errors are discovered is positive, but that they occur in the first place is frightening, and makes one wonder which errors are not found, or worse, not found *in time*. As I will discuss later in this book, one of the ways that death penalty proponents have pushed back against the finding of errors is to make them technically difficult to get to, particularly in federal court.[25]

* * *

By peeking behind the curtain of the post-*Gregg* death penalty system, it is not difficult to find flaws riddling each aspect of modern death sentencing procedure: from the guilt and penalty phases to the complex appellate review procedure. Taken individually, perhaps these flaws would be inconsequential, but where they combine, and where they affect matters of life and death, such flaws strongly undermine the efficacy of the death penalty in America.

Both criminal and civil trials are universally subject to a jurisdiction's rules of evidence. These rules codify the legal profession's general beliefs about what kinds of evidence are reliable for reaching the truth and, consequently, what kinds of evidence are *not* reliable for reaching the truth. Reliable evidence—for instance, testimony given by an eyewitness to relevant events—is admissible at trial, while unreliable evidence—for instance, testimony given by a person who has no knowledge or connection regarding the events at issue—is not admissible. But although these truth-seeking evidentiary rules apply during the guilt phase of death penalty litigation, they are relaxed during the penalty phase.

The rationale for this is that the courts want as much information before the sentence as possible, and view that evidence the way that a normal sentencing would proceed—most sentencing is done based primarily on reports and documents and other forms of hearsay and perhaps a witness or two. It is not uncommon for sentencing information to come in by letter or records or school transcript, and there is not a requirement of a witness with firsthand knowledge to put that evidence in. With the rules being relaxed in a death penalty sentencing hearing, though, there is an "anything-goes" kind of rule on the admission of evidence. Unreliable evidence, which the prosecution could not introduce to prove a defendant's guilt, can be introduced to prove that the defendant's crimes warrant his or her execution. For example, hearsay is normally not allowed to be presented in trial. So someone could not testify that they heard a person on the scene identify a defendant as the murderer. That person who made the identification would have to be presented. But in a penalty hearing, that witness can say exactly that.

Even with the evidence rules in place to ensure that only the most reliable evidence appears during the guilt phase of a capital trial, the success rate of the guilt phase remains highly suspect. Since 1973, 143 death row inmates have received full exoneration (that is, "[a]ll guilt was lifted by the same system that had imposed it in the first place")[26] via post-conviction acquittal, retroactive dismissal of charges, or a governor's pardon in response to the surfacing of new evidence. Of these 143 death row inmates, 123 were convicted under post-*Gregg* procedure that exists largely unchanged today. Although there is no conveniently apparent or readily changeable trend that leads to these erroneous death sentences, the staggering number of American citizens who wrongly sat on death row—including some who were tragically exonerated only *after* they were executed for a crime they did not commit—sufficiently casts doubt on the wisdom of sentencing defendants to death when the procedure for doing so maintains suspect results. One of the most oft-cited tenets of our criminal jurisprudence, espoused by English jurist William Blackstone, is that it is better that ten guilty persons escape, than one innocent suffer.[27] With the error rates in capital convictions, we are falling far short of this ideal.

When these errors occur, a defendant sentenced to death faces significant obstacles to the success of his or her federal habeas corpus petitions. Despite the 40 percent success rate on habeas corpus petitions during the 1973 through 1995 period—mentioned above—in 1996 Congress passed the Antiterrorism and Effective Death Penalty Act (AEDPA), which placed significant limitations on a defendant's access to habeas corpus relief. The Act places the following obstacles on a successful habeas corpus petition: (1) petitions are subject to a one-year statute of limitations, barring defendants from bringing a habeas petition later than one year after the state of conviction's final affirmation of their sentence;[28] (2) appeals of a district court's habeas denial may only occur if the district or a circuit judge issues a "certificate of appealability";[29] (3) petitions may only succeed if the state made an unreasonable factual determination or misapplied a "clearly established" federal law, effectively barring a capital defendant to win habeas relief on a novel legal theory;[30] and (4) strictly regulating the ability to file a second habeas petition after the first petition fails.[31] These obstacles to federal relief deprive many state defendants of a previously available forum for challenging their sentences, even where those defendants may have meritorious claims that were only unsuccessful at the state level for logistical reasons, such as a lack of appointed post-conviction counsel.[32]

Not only are death penalty *procedures* riddled with flaws, but the very rationales that have provided the foundation for the American death penalty since its inception are also being called into question. The efficacy of the death penalty has always been grounded in its presumed ability to effectively deter crime, at the social and individual level, and its retributive ability to punish the worst members of society. Regarding deterrence, however, a multitude of studies conducted from the late 1970s through today have consistently failed to show that the existence of a death penalty has had any impact on deterring crime.[33] This makes some visceral sense. If the robber of a convenience store is thinking about possible punishment at all (rather than his next drug fix, for example) and the store owner resists, that robber will shoot everyone in the place to avoid capture, rather than not shoot to avoid the death penalty.

Indeed, as someone who practices law in Chicago, and who at the beginning of her career watched judges go to jail for taking bribes in Operation Greylord,[34] it is hard to imagine that deterrence has much of a role. After all, if there is someone who ought to know what the consequences of his actions are, it should be a *judge*.

Likewise, many scholars have pointed to the high costs of the death penalty to support the argument that retribution can be more efficiently served by eliminating the death penalty in favor of life terms of imprisonment, and using the financial savings to fund programs to address the mental and social ills that lead many persons to commit crimes. As an example of the costs associated with the death penalty, since 1978 California has spent $4 billion in taxpayer funds to litigate death penalty prosecutions and carry out eventual executions. Because California has only executed thirteen defendants during that time, the cost-per-execution works out to a staggering $308 million.[35] Compared to defendants sentenced to life-terms of imprisonment, sentencing a defendant to death row costs $90,000 more per year. Yet, in both scenarios the defendant remains isolated from society and unable to repeat his or her offenses.

Whether because of the flaws in the guilt and penalty phases of death penalty litigation, the burdensome hurdles to federal habeas corpus, the questionable impact that the death penalty has on deterrence, or the high costs associated with applying the death penalty—from trial through execution, there has been a pronounced shift in attitudes regarding the death penalty in recent years. While seventeen states have officially eliminated the death penalty from their state law, thirteen more have not carried out an execution in at least five years.[36] Likewise, countries all over the world are categorically eliminating the death penalty, to the point where the United States is in the global minority by retaining its death penalty.[37]

Despite the palpable shift in attitudes toward the death penalty, both within the United States and outside of it, there has been no indication that the death penalty is going anywhere in America. In response to these factors, this book will examine the death penalty as it exists today and will aim to answer this fundamental question: what's keeping it alive?

2

MORAL AND RELIGIOUS UNDERPINNINGS OF THE DEATH PENALTY

Although American support for the death penalty has steadily decreased over the years, the death penalty continues to be generally favored and is still sought often, particularly by certain states. What are the factors that have pushed support for the death penalty over the hill in abolitionist states? What has kept the death penalty alive and well in others? These questions are complex, and are discussed throughout this book. At its base, the support for or opposition to the death penalty ultimately stems from views regarding the morality of the death penalty, both abstractly and in practice.

Because the death penalty is ultimately a culmination of abstract and experiential aspects, discussion of the death penalty will necessarily include consideration of ideas and principles as well as of the people who have committed serious crimes, including murder, plotting and carrying out terrorist attacks, and treason; it will almost always also involve discussion about the victims of those crimes. Thus, proponents of the death penalty often include horrific stories of crime and criminality—which are often quite powerful—as their response to an abolitionist position. Similarly, support for or opposition to the death penalty will sometimes involve references to religious doctrines and traditions that influence individuals' ideas about if, or when, the death penalty is acceptable.

In the context of the various components making up the death penalty debate, it is not difficult to see why the American death penalty continues to be a heated topic of debate, with a vast array of views and ideas about its place in society. With the advent of the Internet and our ability to be more in tune with world events, the topic has continued to draw domestic and international attention. Moreover, in the United States, the death penalty debate has continued. Watching the news, reading articles and editorials, and, more recently, reading comments on crime stories online reveals a diverse array of viewpoints, values, and ideas about the morality and acceptability of the death penalty.

So where do all of these ideas come from? And how might we characterize them to better understand our own thoughts and those of others?

Let's start with one category of viewpoints: the utilitarian category. This category of thought includes views that support the death penalty based on a desire to prevent or deter crime, or on a desire to incapacitate offenders who may otherwise continue to commit serious crimes. Utilitarianism, which relies on the utility of a given action to determine its morality, is an outcome-based category of views. Throughout the death penalty's robust history, people ranging from philosophers and politicians to average concerned citizens have used utilitarian arguments to defend the death penalty while others have used them to condemn it. However, in this chapter, we will explore some of the more common arguments in support of the death penalty falling into the utilitarian category of views.

The first of those categories is prevention. Utilitarianism founded in prevention can be illustrated by the frequent statement regarding the death penalty: *if criminals know that the punishment for this crime is the death penalty, they might think twice about committing the crime.* Similar logic extends to theories about criminal punishment in general, but in the death penalty context, the assumption is that the seriousness and finality of the death penalty will force people to give special consideration to the potential death sentence before committing certain crimes. Thus, prevention lies not in the actual usage of the death penalty, but in the mere existence of death penalty legislation for specific crimes. Whether the death penalty effectively prevents the crimes for which it can constitutionally be imposed, however, is still an open and often-debated question.

People operating under utilitarian concepts based on deterrence, on the other hand, will most likely consider the imposition of a death sentence and the effect it will have on the offender, referred to as *specific* deterrence, and others aware of that sentence, or *general* deterrence. Under the paradigm of specific deterrence, offenders sentenced to death will, based on the imposition of the death sentence, no longer engage in the criminal behavior carrying that sentence. In other words, the death sentence will prevent the offender from ever committing another crime, though some may believe that specific deterrence may be achieved by other less severe means, namely life imprisonment.

More commonly, however, people will justify a pro–death penalty stance under the theory of general deterrence. On a basic level, general deterrence is the idea that imposing the death penalty will *send a message* to others and deter them from committing similar crimes. This is a message that, as I will discuss further, is often one of the many sound bites often brought into death penalty debate. Recently, when news broke that the U.S. government would seek the death penalty against Dzhokhar Tsarnaev, one of the Boston Marathon bombers, the reaction from victims' families and law enforcement officials included several individuals hoping to send a message to other potential offenders thinking about engaging in acts of domestic terrorism. Deterrence has long been a rallying cry for the death penalty—even in historical times, the message of general deterrence has woven throughout some of the most (in)famous executions—the executions of Socrates, the slaves of the Spartacus rebellion, Jesus of Nazareth, Marie Antoinette, Patrick Henry, Timothy McVeigh, and Saddam Hussein are just a few.

Incapacitation, another theory of deterrence, necessarily requires not only the imposition of a death sentence, but also the offender's execution. The general idea behind incapacitation is the indisputable fact that executed prisoners cannot, by definition, continue committing serious crimes. One example of incapacitation at play can be seen in many animal control situations where a dog bites an individual and the dog is euthanized: the decision to euthanize does not necessarily encompass whether the dog deserved to die or be punished; rather, it stems from the uncertainty about whether the dog, given similar circumstances, would bite someone again. Although perhaps crude, the example is nevertheless fitting and has been used in the public sphere, even being featured in *The Green Mile*.[1] Similarly, although life imprisonment would incapacitate the offender from continuing to commit crimes outside of prison, many supporters of the death penalty as incapacitation argue that it wouldn't be enough—the lives of other incarcerated individuals, guards, or personnel may still potentially be in danger. Thus, under this view, the death penalty is the only way to ensure that someone will never kill again.

Utilitarian theories encompassing prevention, deterrence, or incapacitation are not new. John Stuart Mill, the quintessential utilitarian, justified the British death penalty using arguments that incorporated each of these concepts in 1868. According to Mill, executing offenders would not only incapacitate the offenders, but would also deter others from committing similar crimes and thus prevent the future harm to other potential victims. To Mill and many of his contemporaries, the death penalty was not just a morally permissible tool, it was a governmental necessity to save countless lives. However, even over one hundred years later, utilitarian views continue to contribute to the death penalty debate. In 2005, after the 1,000th execution since the death penalty was reintroduced in 1976, George W. Bush reaffirmed his solemn support for the death penalty by explaining that it ultimately "helps to save innocent lives" and "serves as a deterrent." A similar sentiment is embodied by the actions of Congress and, today, the Obama administration.[2]

A more recently popular trend, utilitarian in nature, considers not only the danger of recidivism if the offender is not executed, but also the offender's ability to benefit from public funds and services. Under this viewpoint, incapacitation by life imprisonment is inappropriate because money spent in order to house, feed, and care for the medical needs of a capital offender would take away from the government's ability to provide other services for the rest of society. Unlike the more traditional utilitarian grounds of support for the death penalty, the idea that money is better spent executing an offender rather than keeping him in prison for life has not been expounded in an academic sense. Rather, it has generally been confined to a colloquial setting: *why should our tax dollars be used to feed, clothe, and medicate murderers?* Or *why don't we just execute offenders who are clearly guilty of the crime right away in order to save money?* Of course, such statements necessarily misunderstand the aggregate costs of the death penalty, the constitutional ban against cruel and unusual punishment, the role of mitigating factors in capital sentencing schemes, the constitutional guarantee of equal protection for all individuals, and the constitutional guarantee to due process of law. Every study that has looked at the issue has concluded that the death penalty and attendant trial and appeals cost MORE than imprisonment and attendant trial and appeals.[3] However, it is important to acknowledge that these types of views exist because, ultimately, such views may drive movements toward the imposition, reinstatement, or continuation of the death penalty. And these arguments make visceral sense to the public.

Despite the prevalence of utilitarian support for the death penalty, one of the most common justifications of the death penalty stems from the belief that it is a tool to seek retribution for the offender's crimes. According to Immanuel Kant, perhaps one of the most well-known retributivists in the world, once the offender's guilt is established, his punishment should be equivalent to the crime he committed. In other words, offenders who commit serious crimes, most often murder, must be sentenced to death because they *deserve* it—the death penalty is, in a way, an expression of societal moral disapproval at the offender's actions and any of the aggravating factors surrounding those actions.

Retribution is deeply rooted in the history of the death penalty. From biblical times, messages about retribution and otherworldly depictions of the death penalty, justified as godly retribution, have appeared time and time again. The most prevalent, illustrative, and often-quoted biblical call for retribution is found in the Book of Leviticus: "If a man injures his neighbor, what he has done must be done to him: broken limb for broken limb, eye for eye, tooth for tooth. As the injury inflicted, so must be the injury suffered."[4]

Retributive justice in the form of the death penalty can also be seen in numerous biblical stories. For example, after judging the actions of the inhabitants of Earth and finding that only Noah and his family were righteous, God punished everyone else with a deadly flood. Similarly, when Lot offered two angels shelter in his Sodom home, he and his family were spared while the people who went against God's wishes were sentenced to a fiery death by God.[5] Thus, not surprisingly, philosophers, lawmakers, and others have historically relied upon the Jewish Torah or the Christian Old Testament to justify their support for the death penalty despite the commandment, of the ten found in the book of Exodus, that directs the same not to murder.[6] In the United States, the vocal religious factions that often call for the death penalty for serious crimes are the Missouri Synod, the lesser of the two major Lutheran denominations, and the Southern Baptist Convention,[7] the largest Protestant tradition in the world. Although members and factions of other religious organizations commonly found in the United States may also support the death penalty, those organizations, as a whole, tend to lend a more silent support.

Today, retribution remains an important part of the equation in death penalty debates and indeed in jury decisions.

The Supreme Court, in reviewing death penalty cases and laws, has expressly recognized that retribution is a permissible social purpose of the death penalty and has used retributive principles to outlaw the execution of offenders who committed their crimes as juveniles based on their lessened moral blameworthiness. Similarly, capital sentencing hearings are structured in a way that embraces retributivist questions and answers—the measuring of aggravating and mitigating circumstances ultimately goes to whether the offender, judged in a more holistic manner, deserves to be sentenced to death for his or her actions. Outside of the courts, retributive arguments have made an appearance on the national stage through various politicians. For example, during the September 7, 2011, Republican presidential debate held in Simi Valley, California, Texas governor and presidential hopeful Rick Perry was asked about whether he had any difficulties with the 234 capital offenders who had been executed during his gubernatorial term at the time (since then, that number has risen to 269). Without hesitation, Rick Perry said that he never struggled with the executions, explaining:

> [I]n the state of Texas, if you come into our state and you kill one of our children, you kill a police officer, you're involved with another crime and you kill one of our citizens, you will face the ultimate justice in the state of Texas, and that is, you will be executed.[8]

Rick Perry's answer is not only undoubtedly founded in retributivist sentiment that people who engage in those specific crimes deserve the death penalty, but also serves to show that retributive justice in the death penalty can easily lift the burden from the involved decision-makers' shoulders. As Kant would have argued, when the offender deserves the death penalty by way of his criminal actions, the choice to impose the death penalty is out of one's hands after guilt has been established—it is virtually required. As I will address more fully in the following section, the ease with which the actors within the American death penalty machine are able to pass the buck down the line and right back up again is one of the many major criticisms, by abolitionists and others, of the death penalty institution.

Another less publicly endorsed dynamic has also recently become more prominent in death penalty debate: honoring the victim's memory and the victim's family's desire for the oft used (and in the author's view overused) concept of closure. Among the numerous surviving families of homicide victims, there is an irreconcilable divide between those who support the use of the death penalty and those who oppose it. For example, after Timothy McVeigh was caught and tried for the 1995 Oklahoma City bombings, thirty-eight members of victims' surviving families testified during the penalty phase of McVeigh's trial. Over two hundred members of the Oklahoma City bombing victims' families watched McVeigh's execution via closed-circuit television. Yet, right outside the prison walls, members of the Murder Victims' Families for Reconciliation, in conjunction with other groups, held a silent vigil and read a letter written by Bud

Welch, whose twenty-three-year-old daughter was killed in the bombing, protesting the use of the death penalty. While Welch wasn't the only one who did not want the death penalty, he was the most vocal. In his letter, Welch lamented the execution, explaining that McVeigh's death would not bring his daughter back and could possibly lead to more violent retaliation by McVeigh's supporters.

MORAL AND RELIGIOUS CONCEPTS IN ACTION

The moral and religious underpinnings of the death penalty do not exist in a vacuum. Thus, it is important to explore how these concepts are implemented into the death penalty process.

The death penalty is a statutory creation that requires numerous components to pass muster under the federal constitution. In the United States, thirty-two states and the federal government have the death penalty as an available punishment. Eighteen states have abolished the death penalty; the most in our history. Thus, the most significant factor in whether someone will be sentenced to death is ultimately in what jurisdiction he or she is tried. Interestingly, a majority of the states containing large percentages (60+ percent) of people who claimed that religion was "very important" to them during a 2007 Pew Forum survey are, with the exception of West Virginia, death penalty jurisdictions. Over half of the "most religious" death penalty jurisdictions currently have more than fifty people on death row. Moreover, of the eleven former confederate states, nine hold some of the highest numbers of death row inmates and, for Texas, the highest number of executions since 1976 in the country. (I will discuss the importance of the formerly confederate designation in the next section.)

The Southern Baptist Convention, which is vocally pro–death penalty and has a substantial membership mostly concentrated in the southern states, has a large population in almost every "religious" state, in almost every jurisdiction with more than fifty people currently on death row, and in every formerly confederate state. Thus, it is not difficult to see that religious and moral perceptions about the death penalty can have a lasting and important effect on what types of death penalty practices a given jurisdiction has.

If an individual is tried in a death penalty jurisdiction, the next threshold to pass is the nature of the crime with which the alleged offender is charged. In 2008, the Supreme Court held that the death penalty could not be imposed on offenders who were charged with crimes such as the sexual assault or molestation of children because the sentence would be unconstitutionally disproportionate under the Eighth Amendment, nullifying nearly a dozen pieces of legislation that called for the death penalty for those crimes. Thus an offender can be charged with a death-penalty-eligible crime only if it includes murder or possibly treason.

Here is where the rubber meets the road: assuming the alleged offender's crimes are eligible to become a death penalty case, will the prosecutor exercise his or her discretion to seek it? This decision encompasses a number of factors, many of which have to do with the legal requirements of the particular statute based on the required aggravating factors. Aggravating factors are a constitutionally required list of the types of circumstances that, theoretically speaking, change an offense from a run-of-the-mill murder to a murder worthy of the death penalty. Such factors may include the murder of certain types of people, for example, police officers or first responders, murder in specific types of situations such as during the commission of another felony, or malicious murder that has some other horrific aspect in addition to premeditated murder. An often driving, but not generally acknowledged, force in play when deciding whether to pursue the death penalty on a particular case is whether there is public pressure to pursue it. For example, in the case of James Holmes, who walked into an Aurora, Colorado, movie theater on July 20, 2012, during the midnight showing of *The Dark Knight Rises*, and shot into the crowd—killing twelve people and wounding fifty-eight others—there was very strong public and political pressure to seek the death penalty. Sometime in early 2013, Holmes, through his attorneys, offered to plead guilty to all charges in exchange for life in prison. The prosecutors in the case declined Holmes's standing offer. Whether they are continuing to pursue the death penalty based on a retributive sense of necessity to do so, a utilitarian necessity to send mass shooting perpetrators a message that they could be subjected to the death penalty if they try something similar, or simply trying to send a public and political message that they are "tough" on crime, the prosecutors have made the decision that James Holmes should die.

Even if there is no particularly vocal call for the death penalty from the public or the political realm, the decision to seek the death penalty requires prosecutors to engage in value judgments about the offenders and the victims involved in the case. Sometimes, when the case involves a large number of victims, such as the Aurora theater shooting, prosecutors will seek the death penalty because a crime of that magnitude *calls out* for retribution. Similarly, slayings of police officers in the line of duty or slayings of children by a parent, especially a mother, may also fall into the category of crimes that call out for retribution—on one end, it is because the policeman, who was just trying to do his job, represents good, law-abiding society; on the other, it is because our societal and religious norms of women require a high level of commitment and sacrifice from mothers to care for their children, who also often represent innocence, love, and potential.

In this subjective realm, other matters not as noble may enter into the prosecutor's decision. Let me explain what I mean: You may remember career day from high school or junior high. People from various professions would come to the school and speak to you about what you might want to be when you grow up. Well, I have participated in quite a few of those, but the first one I did taught me an important lesson. I was speaking at a junior high school on Chicago's south side, an all-black school. The students listened with barely concealed boredom to the dentist who spoke before me. I was still a public defender at the time, and since I was a part of the Homicide Task Force and defended murder cases, I seemed a bit more interesting to many of them. I finished my talk and asked if there were any questions. A bright seventh-grade girl raised her hand and asked me an extremely interesting question: "When you get a new case," she asked, "what is the first thing you want to know?" The answer spilled out before I thought it through—I recognized its sad truth as I spoke it: "What color is the victim," I said. What was even sadder is that I did not have to explain to any of those junior high school students why that was true. They already knew. Value judgments on which cases "deserve" death are driven in large part by the race and socioeconomic status of the victim. This has been documented by the most rigorous of social science, and it remains a political reality, which I will discuss in more detail in a later chapter.

Apart from value judgments about the people involved, however, a prosecutor must also consider the strength of the case, and his or her ability to convince a jury that the offender should be sentenced to death. For example, if the case involves the murder of an abusive relation and the offender is sympathetic, a prosecutor might decide not to pursue the death penalty for fear of losing at the penalty phase due to the substantial mitigating circumstances, or factors weighing against the imposition of the death penalty. After all, pursuing a death penalty case is extremely expensive and subjects the cases to special rules about the type of staff that should be made available to the defendant, including two lawyers, an investigator, and a mitigation specialist in most jurisdictions. Thus, if the prosecutor has substantial doubts about his or her ability to secure the imposition of the death penalty, he or she might opt not to request that penalty in order to save time and resources for stronger death penalty cases, or at least those cases that have a higher probability of resulting in a death sentence.

Although unconscious biases may play into a death penalty at all stages, the most difficult biases to examine deal with juries. Juries are comprised of twelve people with distinct personalities, worldviews, religious beliefs, and moral compasses. When it comes to death penalty juries, each juror must be willing to impose the death penalty upon a defendant, if they feel that the aggravating circumstances outweigh the mitigating circumstances of the case, even if they are generally opposed to the death penalty.[9] However, in practice, most prosecutors would likely want to remove jurors with reservations about the death penalty. Similarly, though it is more difficult to find such jurors, any jurors who will impose the death penalty in all cases regardless of the value of the mitigating circumstances presented to them should be removed.[10] This process is called "death-qualifying" the jury. Thus, from the very beginning of a trial, the voices of morality that oppose the use of the death penalty, either based on its structure or as a matter of course, have been silenced and removed from a death penalty jury.

Even after death-qualification, jurors' individual ideas of morality will influence the rest of the proceedings at trial and during sentencing. Like the prosecutors who decided to seek the death penalty at the outset of the case, jurors will make judgments about the defendant, the victim, and the circumstances of the crime. Moreover, jurors' moral and religious beliefs may actually affect, whether consciously or subconsciously, the way that jurors interpret the evidence—this ranges from who they believe on the stand, to what theories make sense to them based on their own understanding of the world, to whether they perceive the defendant as dangerous or evil, and whether they do, in fact, interpret the presented evidence of mitigating circumstances as mitigating rather than "excuses." The defendant's image, or portrayal of him or herself, is extremely important because the penalty phase of a death penalty case is ultimately about allowing the jury to look at who the defendant is and empathize with him.

When jurors are afraid of the defendant, either because they think he is dangerous or maybe even evil, it prevents them from evaluating the defendant as a multifaceted human being. Thus, if a juror comes from a religious tradition that categorizes criminals into a sphere of evil or otherness, those religious views might affect the outcome of the case for the defendant.

Perhaps one of the most difficult aspects of death penalty work is trying to explain to jurors *why* the mitigating evidence matters: why does it matter that the defendant was raised by a mother who was addicted to crack cocaine? Why does it matter that the defendant was bullied? Why does it matter that the defendant suffered from mental illness? Why is he, perhaps, less culpable than someone who did not have to deal with that type of adversity in his life? The answers to these types of questions are, unsurprisingly, often connected to the jurors' moral and religious views. People whose moral or religious traditions require them to contemplate the general deterrence of a death sentence may be less open to giving any mitigating evidence strong consideration because of the message they want to send. Similarly, people who are concerned with "doing justice for the victim" may also choose not to give too much weight to the mitigating evidence presented during sentencing. Moreover, when the sentence is announced, jurors who believe that God will take care of anything that needs to be taken care of, or those who believe that the defendant was ultimately the one who imposed the death penalty on himself, might never think twice about the imposition of the sentence.[11]

Consequently, for defense attorneys, the death penalty world can potentially be a world of hostility and melancholy. As mentioned in the previous section, the death penalty realm often involves serious, violent, and gruesome factual circumstances and is often accompanied by serious tension and resentment from the victims' surviving families. It only takes a cursory search of news media coverage of well-known death penalty attorneys to find pages of materials condemning their defense of some of the alleged offenders and sometimes even resorting to ad hominem attacks toward them personally. However, many defense attorneys are not just found "repulsive" in the court of public opinion, but are also similarly treated when representing their clients in court. Although most judges treat prosecution and defense counsel in death penalty cases fairly well, some judges may become hostile with defense attorneys who are trying to zealously advocate for their clients. For example, in 2013, the Alliance for Justice filed a judicial complaint against a federal judge sitting on the United States Court of Appeals for the Fifth Circuit in New Orleans, Edith Jones, after she made racist comments about black and Hispanic offenders' predisposition to "commit acts of violence" and continually put down lawyers who tried to file motions on behalf of their capital clients or claim mental impairment to prevent their clients' unlawful executions. Judge Jones, a strong proponent of the death penalty who has proposed expediting executions by setting a "lenient" schedule of four to six executions per month, reportedly told a crowd of students and attorneys that she was disgusted by capital defendants who claimed retardation.[12] Perhaps more alarmingly, after an attorney filed a new habeas corpus petition based on the Supreme Court's agreement to hear a similar case—and where that resolution might have meant that defendant would not be executed, Judge Jones admonished the attorney for "delay[ing] the law enforcement process," further stating that

> [C]ounsel who have engaged in delaying tactics should be struck from the rolls of the Fifth Circuit and not be allowed to practice in [their] court for a period of years.

[She] would not rule out the imposition of other sanc-
tions as well [because] [a] condemned man's life and society's interest in enforcing the death penalty justly are
matters too important to leave to procedural games.[13]

Judge Jones then compared the attorney's conduct, filing
a habeas corpus petition, to the crimes his client was convicted of—the robbery, rape, and homicide of two people—
and accused him of piercing "[t]he veil of civility."[14] Although the capital defense lawyer was attempting to save his
client's life based on possibly new grounds, Judge Jones had
developed serious animosity toward not only defendants, but
their attorneys.

REDEMPTION ON DEATH ROW AND OTHER CRITICISMS OF THE DEATH PENALTY

Stanley "Tookie" Williams was the founder of the infamous
Los Angeles gang the Crips. In 1981, Williams was sentenced to death for the murders of four people. During his
time on death row, Williams made numerous public statements calling for an end to gang violence, had written nine
anti-gang books, and had volunteered, over the phone, for
several organizations working to deter others from joining or
continuing their affiliations with gangs. According to ac-
counts from his attorney, his supporters, and religious lead-
ers who worked with him, Williams's time on death row had
helped shape a new man who was ready and willing to continue his anti-gang ministry. With a large base of support,

Williams and his attorney petitioned then California govern-
or Arnold Schwarzenegger for a commutation of Williams's
death sentence based on his redemption during the twenty-
five years he was incarcerated on death row. When Governor
Schwarzenegger declined to grant the clemency, the United
States found itself in the midst of a familiar, but heated,
debate about the role that redemption should play after an
offender is placed on death row. The debate ranged from
whether it was possible to have sincere redemption after
committing such horrible crimes to whether sincere redemption is an adequate basis to set aside the death penalty.

The debate about redemption is important because it requires deep thought about why the death penalty is in place
at all—if it is in place as a retributive tool to punish based on
the individual's culpability at the time of the offense and
sentencing, any redemption after the imposition of the death
sentence, no matter how sincere, may be ignored without
consequence. One well-known retributivist philosopher, St.
Thomas Aquinas, believed that, from a moral and religious
perspective, the death penalty was a tool that was designed
to lead sinners onto the road to redemption. To Aquinas, and
other contemporary supporters of the death penalty, the
prospect of the execution is what ultimately helps offenders
make peace with their criminal conduct. Further, Aquinas
believed that execution itself redeemed offenders who had
not redeemed themselves by the time of their death. Thus,
although he believed redemption was important, he did not

believe that reaching it before execution made any difference in the offender's culpability.

Similarly, if the death penalty's purpose is to deter crime in a general matter, one could argue, as some did while Governor Schwarzenegger was considering Williams's petition for commutation, that a commutation of a reformed or redeemed offender would send the wrong message to other people—if you are a murderer, you can escape the death penalty by finding faith or purpose on death row. However, if the death penalty is in place for incapacitation or specific deterrence, sincere redemption would be absolutely relevant and should require a stay of execution or even a commutation of sentence. A sincerely redeemed individual, by definition, would have been deterred from recidivism of the crimes that landed him on death row; moreover, the redeemed individual would no longer pose a threat to society and thus would not warrant the permanent incapacitation that comes with execution.

Although these debates have happened many times since the reinstatement of the death penalty by a majority of the states in 1976, none of the commuted death sentences have been attributed to the offender's rehabilitation or redemption. Accordingly, religious organizations such as the American Baptist Churches, the United States Conference of Catholic Bishops, the United Methodist Church, the Episcopal Church, and the American Jewish Committee, as well as secular organizations such as the National Coalition to Abolish the Death Penalty, have argued that a death sentence denies people the ability or incentive to redeem themselves in their own eyes and the eyes of their societies.

Other common criticisms about the death penalty are, unfortunately, also onerous. One of the most publicized criticisms of the American death penalty is that the legal system continues operating under the possibility of wrongfully convicting innocent people even in death cases. In fact, at least twenty-three of the two-hundred-seventy-three commutations and four pardons of death sentences since 1976 have been explicitly attributed to the doubt about the offender's guilt or the offender's possible innocence. Although that number constitutes only slightly over 8 percent of all of the commutations, many people have argued that the possible execution of a single innocent offender is too great a risk. Moreover, the 8 percent figure does not account for commutations that were granted without explicit reasons or former Illinois governor George Ryan's mass commutation in 2003 of 167 death row inmates. Ryan was swayed in part by the exonerations of four men who had been sentenced to death after falsely confessing under torture overseen by the disgraced former Chicago Police Department commander Jon Burge. Much later, Burge was convicted of three counts of obstruction of justice and perjury after he lied about his participation in torture during a civil lawsuit.[15] Since the death penalty was reinstated in 1976 by several states, there have been at least 143 exonerations of death row inmates. Moreover, at least ten men have been executed despite their possible innocence.[16]

Another alarming concern that continues is the issue of racial bias in charging and sentencing of death penalty cases, as I said above. However, I will address this in more detail in a future chapter.

The last complaint about the death penalty that I will mention during this section deals with the way the death penalty machine is built. At the foundation are the people who, at the state and federal level, vote for the legislators who draft death penalty legislation, then Congress, then the gubernatorial or presidential office. These actors may think that despite any minor problems with the legislation, the next actors will make sure that executions only occur when everything has been done correctly, and the crime or criminal deserve it. Once we get past the foundation, however, we have the prosecutors who seek the death penalty and the judges who do not preclude the prosecution from doing so. Prosecutors and judges might think that, despite any infirmities in the case they present or preside over, the trial and jury process will ensure the integrity of the result. Most likely, the death-qualified jurors will be sure they've made the right decision based on the information they have, which may have included information they received, or did not receive, impermissibly or due to the ineffective assistance of the defendant's lawyer. However, even if there are jurors with doubts, they might ultimately give in under the belief that if they have made a mistake, a higher court can sort everything out. So as the case goes through the system, each actor is relying on what the psychologists call diffused responsibility and assumes that the jury has made a solemn and rational decision, the prosecutors have acted with integrity, the judge has ruled correctly at trial, and defense counsel did everything he or she was supposed to and had the resources to do so. The reviewing courts give significant deference to the judges', lawyers', and jurors' determinations. Come execution day, it is entirely possible that none of the actors involved in sending the offender to death row have really come to terms with the fact that they have actively and *personally* sent the offender to his death.

This sense of diffused responsibility makes it difficult to see one's active role in the death of a capital offender. That fact can be seen more clearly when one considers some of the built-in safeguards in the administration of the death penalty. For example, when Utah executed Ronnie Lee Gardner by firing squad in 2010, five men stood behind a wall armed with rifles—four of which contained live rounds. One of the marksmen's rifles was loaded with wax bullets instead. However, in order for all of the marksmen involved to retain some doubt over whether they fired the shot that ultimately killed Gardner, none of the marksmen knew whose rifle contained the wax bullets. Moreover, any doctors, nurses, or correctional officers involved in executions by lethal injections cannot be publicly identified. Although this secrecy is partly based on the concern that participants' safety could be affected by identification, it also prevents the execution team from having to be confronted about their choice of work unless they publicly announce it on their own.

Jerry Givens, a former Virginia executioner who has come out against the death penalty after participating in the executions of sixty-two people, has described some of the mystique involved with carrying out executions for the state—which, at the time, he rationalized by reminding himself that the men he was executing had condemned themselves through their foolish actions.[17] Thus, at the end of the line, even the person who pulls the trigger or switch, injects the poison, or ties the knot may not appreciate that they've just killed someone without qualifying it with "maybe it wasn't my bullet." Of course it's everybody's bullet.

3

THE MEDIA AS A MESSENGER
OF DEATH

The criminal justice system, and in particular the criminal defense bar, has always had a complex relationship with the media. There are competing parts of the Constitution to consider, namely, the First and the Sixth Amendments. Generally speaking, publicity hurts a criminal defendant and helps the prosecution, although there are times where the opposite is true.[1]

The First Amendment to the Constitution, which guarantees freedom of the press, has been a historically coveted right. However, First Amendment interests can sometimes conflict directly with a defendant's right to a fair trial and an impartial jury, particularly in capital cases. Freedom of the press, while essential, can and often does skew the public's view of an accused person. Thus, a defendant's Sixth Amendment guarantees, namely that he will be judged by a jury of his peers based only on the evidence presented to them, is difficult to preserve under the glare of biased and one-dimensional reporting.

For the defense, there are already so many presumptions against anyone charged—particularly anyone charged with a violent offense. Most jurors walk into court with these presumptions: where there's smoke there's fire, the police wouldn't arrest someone who hadn't done it, and of course— he isn't one of *us*, is he?

For the prosecution there is the expectation that they are on the side of the angels, that they will always be successful, and an inordinate amount of pressure to never express doubt or, worse, sympathy toward the defense.

Although the media's sensational coverage regarding crime, trials, and the death penalty may seem like a newer phenomenon (with dedicated channels such as CourtTV and shows like *Law and Order*), the media has been a close companion of criminal trials since colonial times. As early as the 1700s, "American" newspapers picked up stories about crime, trials, and sometimes even covered then-public executions.[2] In the late 1800s and early 1900s, when newspapers were accompanied by radio and television, the "trial by tabloid" became a more serious problem—one that Supreme Court Chief Justice William Howard Taft called "[t]he greatest evil and the most vicious one."[3]

However, despite any of the media's evils when it comes to criminal trials, the love-hate relationship between First Amendment and Sixth Amendment guarantees is uniquely codependent. Without freedom of the press in judicial proceedings, the courts would have little accountability in litigation matters, including those involving freedom of the press—in fact, the press must often rely on the judiciary to strike down any laws limiting its access to information or to enforce laws, such as the Freedom of Information Act, that grant them such access to that information. Similarly, through their Sixth Amendment guarantee to a public trial, many defendants often rely on the press to expose unfair practices in the judiciary. In the well-known case of Emmett Till, the Chicago teen who was tortured and murdered in Mississippi after he whistled at a white woman, the media ultimately exposed the killers' graphic and gleeful confessions after being acquitted of murder charges by an all-white, all-male Mississippi jury.[4]

More recently, even though it was a long time coming, former Chicago Police Department commander Jon Burge would never have gone to jail for the torture of those he arrested without the intervention of the press and the assiduity of a few lawyers and reporters.

So what roles does the media actually play in the context of criminal trials? The mass media is an arbiter of chaos. Tasked with reporting complex situations within narrow time and space constraints, the media turns "news" into "news stories"; it translates events involving real-life human beings into digestible narratives involving heroes, villains, and moral dichotomies of right and wrong.

While such stories are rarely outright false, they nevertheless shape the framework through which media consumers view a particular topic. When media outlets cover violent crimes, they usually do not portray suspects, victims, and law enforcement officials; instead, they portray heroes (law enforcement officials), villains (suspects), and tragic figures (victims). By the time the trial begins, the narrative treatment of the underlying crime has been established, and the public has grown hungry to see the villain's downfall—even when that downfall is execution.

When it comes to media coverage, not every capital case is equal, however. The media has historically focused on distinct breeds of death penalty cases emblematic of an era's sociopolitical climate. In the roaring twenties, the media focused on death penalty cases implicating wealth. In the Depression era through World War II, media coverage spun xenophobic narratives for newsworthy crimes. The "moral panic" of the 1970s saw the rise of the serial killer in the public consciousness. The current generation of media-frenzy death penalty cases has seen a more fundamental shift, marked by the arrival of "Twitter reporting," where social networks and online forums create a media landscape where millions of content providers can weigh in on high-profile cases.

Widely considered the first high-profile death penalty case of the mass media era, the 1924 Leopold and Loeb murder trial captured the collective attention of an America firmly in the grip of the glamour and excess of the roaring twenties. Leopold and Loeb were young, wealthy, and prodigiously intelligent; they believed themselves to be intellec-

THE MEDIA AS A MESSENGER OF DEATH

tual "supermen" capable of crafting the perfect undetectable crime; and their victim was the son of an influential Chicago millionaire. During both the investigation and ensuing trial, the media fed the public's appetite for details of the unusual crime. And when Leopold and Loeb's attorney, Clarence Darrow, delivered a rousing twelve-hour closing argument that passionately attacked the death penalty and ultimately spared his clients' lives, it was reported verbatim in newspapers nationwide. Due to the media's heavy coverage of the Leopold and Loeb trial, Darrow's words were immortalized by the press and remain influential to anti–death penalty advocates to this day.[5]

Less than ten years later, America was in the midst of the Great Depression. While the government responded to the Depression by adopting nationalist economic policies, jobless Americans responded with bitter xenophobia. So in 1932 when a German immigrant, "Bruno" Richard Hauptmann, was accused of kidnapping and murdering famed aviator Charles Lindbergh's baby, the media covered the proceedings incessantly. The press dubbed the murder "the Crime of the Century" and portrayed Hauptmann as a foreign outsider. In the light cast by the media, he was no mere criminal suspect, he was a non-American aggressor; his crime affected more than just Lindbergh and his family, it affected the entire country. Unsurprisingly, given the media coverage and the social climate at the time, Hauptmann was convicted and executed, though historians continue to debate his actual guilt.[6]

The 1960s had seen both the rise of the counterculture movement and a dramatic increase in the rate of violent crime across the country. Drawing a correlation between the two trends, large segments of the population feared that the country was spiraling into a pit of moral decay. In the 1970s, as politicians vowed to restore the country to law and order, the media took increasing interest in the trials of serial killers. Reporting incessantly about Charles Manson, John Wayne Gacy, Ted Bundy, and others, the media reinforced America's fear of violent crime by constantly reminding consumers that serial killers walk among them, while simultaneously relieving those fears by assuring consumers that the killers will be caught and punished to the full extent of the law—which was, frequently, execution. Thus, the criminal defense bar was also dealing with old but evolving problems in media coverage—where only newspaper articles were once written, television news stories began to appear alongside them, intensifying the effects of the media coverage on any given case.

Unsurprisingly, by the 1970s, the police drama had already begun to grow into one of the most popular types of shows in the United States, growing exponentially by the 1990s.[7] By 1994, the world was enthralled, in an astounding parallel to the hangings that took place in colonial times, by the O. J. Simpson trial, which featured everything good ratings call for: romance, murder, and a nationally recognized football player.[8] Although the Simpson trial would end with several courts' disenchantment with televised trials, it did not end America's love affair with crime as entertainment.[9]

Following the Simpson trial, television news outlets also began to substantially increase their crime coverage. Thus, even though U.S. crime rates were declining, the public saw more stories about crimes in 1995 than it did when crime rates were approximately 13 percent higher only five years prior.[10] The media's continued infatuation with crime as entertainment, beyond flooding the nightly news with crime stories, has also led to the continued blurring between nonfiction news and quasifictional storytelling. These new quasifictional programs, in the style of a documentary, generally have dramatizations, flashbacks, and detectives telling the stories based on their perception of the evidence.[11] Today, these programs continue to be widely popular—in fact, Investigation Discovery, a channel founded in 1996, dedicates the bulk of its programming to shows either "following" detectives or having them recount their experiences with old cases.[12] As I will explain in more detail below, these developments carry important consequences in the context of real trials by shaping juror expectations and perceptions of crimes, criminals, and justice.

Since the beginning of the new millennium, Internet culture has changed how the American public interacts with the media and, correspondingly, with the trials that make headlines. No longer are Americans only passive media consumers. In the age of Twitter and online blogging, media consumers have become media creators. And nowhere was this shift more pronounced than in the 2011 Casey Anthony trial. Anthony was charged with—and ultimately acquitted of— the murder of her daughter, Caylee. The traditional media initially took interest in the case, but it was Twitter and Facebook that ultimately earned the trial the moniker of "Social Media Trial of the Century." From news outlets live-tweeting the trial as it progressed to online articles compiling Twitter and Facebook reactions to the not guilty verdict, online platforms gave everybody an opportunity to weigh in on the case. It remains to be seen what the lasting impact of social media will have on death penalty trials in the future, but if the Casey Anthony trial provided any insight at all, it revealed the mob mentality that individuals adopt when commenting on a high-profile defendant's guilt or innocence.

How is it that publicity becomes pervasive in one case and not another? In some situations, where the offender and/or the complaining witness are already famous, the answer seems obvious, such as in the many cases against Lindsay Lohan,[13] or the charges against Michael Jackson's physician.[14] But other cases take on lives of their own, like that of my former client, Casey Anthony,[15] or the notorious Susan Smith. On October 25, 1994, Smith reported to police that she had been carjacked by a black man who drove away with her sons still in the car. For nine days, she made dramatic pleas on national television for the rescue and return of her children. However, following an intensive investigation and a nationwide search, on November 3, 1994, Smith confessed to letting her car roll into nearby John D. Long Lake, drowning her children inside. Smith's defense psychiatrist diagnosed her with dependent personality disorder and major depression. Her biological father committed suicide when she was six years old, and she rarely had a stable home life. It was disclosed in her trial that Smith was molested in her teens by her stepfather, who not only admitted to it, but also revealed that he had consensual sex with her as an adult. At thirteen, she attempted suicide. After graduating from high school in 1989, she made a second attempt to end her own life. Susan married David Smith and had the two children, but the relationship was rocky due to mutual allegations of infidelity, and the couple separated several times. Smith was in a relationship with a wealthy man named Tom Findlay who did not want children in his life. She killed her children in order to be able to continue the relationship and so that he would look after her. Although the state asked for the death penalty, the jury sentenced her to life in prison.[16]

There is no question that when publicity is present, there is what is colloquially referred to as "heat" on the case, which makes the case much more challenging for all concerned. If, for example, the prosecution comes to believe that a reduction in charges, or even a dismissal, is appropriate, it is harder to take that action in the glare of the media. It is also very difficult for a judge—particularly a judge who runs for election—to remain impervious to the public scrutiny, and as one of my clients once told me, "A judge don't get in no trouble for locking up somebody, but he sure get in trouble for letting him go." In other words, and as I will discuss further in the next chapter, it is much "safer" politically to accede to the prosecution's requests and look "tough on crime."

I have been involved in some high-profile death penalty cases, and as a result, I have personally confronted as well as observed the pervasive intrusion of the news media into the criminal justice system. In these cases, news media begins to mirror the tabloids.[17] In states such as Florida, Mississippi, Nevada, and Oregon, where cameras are allowed in court, this influence is even more pronounced.[18] It has had profound effects on the nature of prosecutions, poisoning of potential jury pools, the quality of the defense, and judicial decision making.[19] Cameras in the courtroom have also given rise to legal commentators, most of whom have a partisan political view and are willing, frankly, to do and say anything at all to be on television.[20] Putting on a show for the news media provokes commentators and encourages further misrepresentation of criminal cases that ultimately affects almost every aspect of the accused's case.

It is not just the parties that have something at stake in these cases. The lead defense attorney for my former client, Casey Anthony, poses a striking example. In the weeks leading up to and during the Anthony trial, Jose Baez was the subject of lengthy commentary.[21] Beyond attempting to deconstruct Baez's courtroom performance, the media has prodded at his past career experiences, his personal life, and how the Anthony ruling might affect his future.[22] This type of irrelevant and often speculative reporting forces criminal defense lawyers to take this coverage into account in their strategy—using jury selection to ask potential jurors about what media coverage they have seen, requesting additional jury instructions that reiterate the prohibition on extrajudicial research, and so on. Unlike private firms with public relations budgets, most criminal defendants are poor, and thus the criminal defense attorney must conduct his or her own media management in addition to actually trying the case. Thus, part of what an attorney in a high-publicity case needs to take into account is legal commentary which, as I have written before, is given a great deal of weight without the benefit of meaningful regulations to hold them accountable to.[23]

In a death penalty case, the media's involvement becomes much more intrusive and dangerous. Media pressure in death penalty cases can potentially make the difference between life and death—strong media involvement in a case may mean that the prosecutors charging the case are not "free" to accept a plea of guilty in exchange for taking the death penalty off the table. Moreover, because the media affects how we perceive crime,[24] the accused, and the players in the system,[25] media involvement early on in a case may make the difference between what crime is charged or, in non–death penalty cases, *whether the crime is charged at all.* Based on the strong influence of media portrayals of criminality on actual law enforcement, particularly of criminality in certain demographic groups, the portrayals defined by age, gender, socioeconomic group, and race have been decried by many. [26] After all, jurors, prosecutors, and defense attorneys are not the only people who are exposed to these portrayals—law enforcement officers, voters, and legislators are also exposed to them and may draw certain conclusions from them.

Not surprisingly, if you ask most people where they get their information about the criminal justice system, they most likely won't say the court system, but may also be as unlikely to say that they get it from newspapers, civics classes, or even news magazines. Most likely, they will say that they get their information from the local news and television programs—in particular the ubiquitous and long-running *Law and Order* television program and its spinoffs. [27]

These programs have predictable qualities to them—there is a victim, and a bad guy (the "perp"), and the forces of good who arrest or exact revenge on the two-dimensional bad guy. [28] The victim is also two-dimensional. [29] She is pure as the driven snow, or too young to have discernable faults. [30]

What does this mean in the context of jury selection? Jury selection in a capital case is far more complicated and difficult than in an ordinary case. [31] *Witherspoon v. Illinois* [32] states that the prosecution in a capital case has the right to exclude, for cause, anyone who could not consider giving the death penalty. *Adams v. Texas,* [33] as interpreted in *Wainwright v. Witt,* [34] modified the "automatic" and "unmistakably clear" language of *Witherspoon's* footnotes 9 and 21, which allowed the exclusion for cause only when a juror unqualifiedly expressed his or her unwillingness to consider the death penalty.[35] This changed the dynamics of jury selection by making it easier for the prosecution to exclude for cause, but it also complicated matters—jurors who are "substantially impaired" by virtue of anti–capital punishment views must be identified. Second, jurors who are "substantially impaired" by virtue of *pro*–capital punishment views must be identified.[36] Third, venire members must be identified who are substantially impaired *in considering lawful mitigating evidence.*[37]

From the defense perspective, the negative effects of death-qualification and excluding people opposed to the death penalty increase the likelihood of conviction and of decisional errors.[38] Because a defendant in a capital case has a right to an impartial jury for capital sentencing as well as for trial under the Constitution,[39] which includes the right to an adequate voir dire to permit the identification of unqualified jurors,[40] voir dire should be sufficient to gather adequate information about prospective jurors' beliefs and opinions so as to allow removal of those members of the venire whose minds are so closed by bias and prejudice that they cannot apply the law as instructed in accordance with their oath.

That's a laudable goal, but difficult to accomplish, and the narrative created in the media makes it all the more difficult—and not just for the defense.

Part of the reason is that jurors come in to service with a point of view; when a juror comes into a courtroom, he does so with certain scripts in his head.[41] His life experiences, his upbringing, and his education all help him to function in the world, and that means that he expects certain events to happen a certain way. If the traffic light turns green, it means you can go, right? A potential juror walks into a courthouse with expectations about crime, courts, and criminals—but his life experiences, upbringing, and education are not necessarily where he gets those expectations. In all likelihood he has little or no contact with the criminal justice system personally, has not studied it in school, and wasn't brought up around folks with personal or educational knowledge about it. So where will those expectations come from? The news and television crime drama, that's where.[42]

Even assuming our juror has no particular political viewpoint about crime, has no hidden agendas, and is otherwise a blank slate, social science tells us that he will believe that "dark is dangerous,"[43] that the police always get the right guy, and that the prosecutors are knights in shining armor.[44] Or he may come into the courtroom believing that police all lie, that the prosecution is always motivated by venal desires, and that the entire system cannot be trusted. Even if this hypothetical juror intellectually knows better, the only *stories* he has heard on the subject are from these sources, not from his own experience or that of anyone close to him. The potential juror's life history is not likely to help him look critically at the news or at crime drama, and he will likely be unaware consciously of its effect upon him.[45] It becomes important for the courts and practitioners to be aware of and allow for real inquiry into these matters if the constitutional protections are to be adhered to in a death penalty case.

I do not wish to end this chapter without again talking about how the media can and has also played an important positive role for the accused, crime victims, and the abolition of the death penalty. Had it not been for the *Chicago Tribune*'s series on the death penalty in 1999,[46] it is unlikely that former governor George Ryan would have placed a moratorium on executions[47] and ultimately commuted all of those sentenced to death to life without parole before leaving office.[48] It was Ryan's actions, as well as the sea change in attitudes toward the death penalty, that caused Illinois ultimately to abolish the death penalty.[49]

4

THE DEATH PENALTY AS
A POLITICAL TOOL

The death penalty serves many purposes. For example, in the view of its proponents, it serves as a deterrent, despite the fact that no study supports this view. In the view of its opponents, the only purpose of the death penalty is to turn the state and the justice system into murderers.

In this chapter I examine another "use" of the death penalty—the political one. Before I delve into this, there is one caveat: the members of the prosecution and defense teams seldom view themselves as political actors. They are concerned with their case(s), and what they view as the just result. When asked to step back and view the political impact of the death penalty, most cannot. The head of a prosecutor's office can and may do so consciously, a trial or appellate judge—especially one who is elected—may do so as well; but generally those of us "on the ground" defending or prosecuting an individual person do not usually see that political world. We are immersed in the details of the crime, in trying to tell the defendant's story or to defeat or overwhelm it in some way, and while we may notice the press and the public are interested, we often ignore the impact of that interest.

When I teach at death penalty defense seminars, I am often asked to lecture on motions practice. Motions practice in death penalty cases is very specialized and of great import. As I have discussed before,[1] a major reason for the defense to file and litigate motions is to win them, of course (the prosecution tends to file fewer "opening motions" and is generally responding to those filed by the defense). The defense lawyer hopes that the confession will not come in, that the eyewitness will not be allowed to point the finger at the defense lawyer's client, that the hearsay about the defendant isn't admitted at trial, or that the judge agrees that this should not be a death case. And sometimes, the defense actually *wins* these motions. But often the defense does not, and it becomes discouraging for the defense to continue to file and litigate them, particularly in an unfriendly forum, or due to a large caseload.

Nonetheless, the defense lawyer should file any motion for which there is a good faith basis. The defense lawyer should do this because it is the right thing to do for the defendant, because it might just work, and very importantly, because it may indeed lay the groundwork for a successful appeal. If the defense lawyer does not object to improper evidence or trial conduct, it is almost certainly waived for appellate purposes. Worse yet, if the defense lawyer doesn't do it in the right *way*, she has almost certainly insulated the error from federal review.

This is especially true in a capital case because there is no way to anticipate what motion or objection that courts have thus far deemed as unworthy may ultimately lay the groundwork for a successful attack in the future.

The defense lawyer also needs to pay attention to making the record during the trial itself. The defense lawyer needs to make objections, of course, but also to be careful not to "unmake" them by appearing to accede to the judge's ruling. For example, if the defense lawyer objects to a photograph's introduction into evidence and the objection is overruled, he should not say "okay, your Honor." Instead, he should carefully try to say something nonoffensive, such as, "I understand your ruling." Increasingly state courts are following the federal lead and avoiding issues by finding them waived when they can.

Why is this federalizing important? After all, the writ of habeas corpus seems to most defense attorneys some arcane thing that "federal" attorneys do to fix what went wrong in state court that resulted in imprisonment or a death sentence for their client. Similarly, it is not on the radar for most prosecutors either. It seems far removed and relatively unimportant in the preparation of a case for trial. Trial lawyers, particularly defense attorneys, certainly understand how important it is to preserve the record, to object, and to state both the state and federal grounds for the objection. But what is not immediately apparent is how, working backward, the Antiterrorism and Effective Death Penalty Act of 1996 (AEDPA) has altered and intensified not only the need to preserve the record, but the *manner* in which it must be done. In fact, the AEDPA can be seen as providing the support and justification for an expanded motions practice, evidentiary hearings, and discovery.

Before the AEDPA, it could certainly be argued that a conscientious defense attorney should file and litigate motions where she had (at least) more than a suspicion or a hunch that such a motion was necessary. For instance, she would not file a motion to dismiss the charges based on allegations of prosecutorial misconduct unless she had very solid evidence of that misconduct, and that conduct was sufficiently egregious to warrant such a motion. Indeed, even if it *were* that egregious, she might decide, for reasons of trial strategy or because she thought the motion unlikely to succeed, not to file it. She could do so, secure in the knowledge that should more evidence come to light later on, and it was evidence that she could not have reasonably located through the exercise of due diligence, such a challenge could be mounted in a federal habeas corpus proceeding.[2] That simply is no longer the case unless the prosecutorial misconduct is of such a nature that not only could one show prejudice to the court (a difficult enough endeavor), but innocence of the crime itself.[3]

In other words, if the defense attorney has any reason at all to file such a motion she must do so. The price of failing to do so is that the issue almost never can be brought to the attention of the federal court unless it is accompanied by proof of actual innocence. This certainly increases the burden on the defense attorney. To fail to object, to file a motion, or to elicit a fact from a witness may indeed prove literally fatal later to your client's ability to even talk about the issue to a federal court. It is a daunting and frightening prospect.

So what does this have to do with politics? Well, I often start a lecture on motions practice with this tongue-in-cheek comment: the first motion I file in a death penalty case is a motion to continue this to an uneven-numbered year. That is because no defense lawyer wants her case to be a part of any judge or prosecutor's re-election campaign.

Recently, this issue was discussed by United States Supreme Court Justice Sonia Sotomayor in the case of *Woodward v. Alabama*.[4] The death row inmate in that case was asking the United States Supreme Court to hear his case. This is called a petition for certiorari—it's essentially a request that the highest court in our country hear the case and decide an issue the petitioner believes needs to be decided by the highest court in the country. So in addition to the reason the petitioner thinks his case has merit, he must also convince the United States Supreme Court that it is of national importance. Most of these petitions are denied, as was this one. What was unusual was that Justice Sotomayor wrote a lengthy dissent about the denial. The dissent is all about politics, and how they interact—quite visibly—with the death penalty in Alabama. As I mentioned earlier, I will tell you about this in some detail, and then turn my attention to the politics that are a bit more difficult to see. A death penalty case is really two trials. First, it's a trial on the merits (Did your client commit the crime? If he did, was it first-degree murder?). In some jurisdictions, the question of eligibility for the death penalty is answered at the trial on the merits. As I've previously mentioned, this means that in order for the prosecution to even ask for the death penalty, it must prove a first-degree murder as well as an aggravating factor that takes the case into the (allegedly) small group of cases where the death penalty can even be sought. A common aggravating factor that makes a first-degree murder case into a capital case is the first-degree murder of a police officer acting in the line of duty, or a first-degree murder of a woman during a rape.

Assuming the prosecution is able to establish both guilt and eligibility beyond a reasonable doubt, the jury then decides whether death is the appropriate choice of punishment. In all but a few states the sentencing decision is entirely the jury's to make. As Justice Sotomayor notes:

> Of the 32 States that currently authorize capital punishment, 31 require jury participation in the sentencing decision; only Montana leaves the jury with no sentencing role in capital cases. . . . In 27 of those 31 States, plus the federal system, . . . the jury's decision to impose life imprisonment is final and may not be disturbed by the trial judge under any circumstance. That leaves four States in which the jury has a role in sentencing but is not the final decision maker. In Nebraska, the jury is responsible for

finding aggravating circumstances, while a three-judge
panel determines mitigating circumstances and weighs
them against the aggravating circumstances to make the
ultimate sentencing decision. . . . Three States—Alabama, Delaware, and Florida—permit the trial judge to
override the jury's sentencing decision. (Citations omitted)[5]

There was another state with a jury override—Indiana—
but it changed its law in 2004. In Mr. Woodward's case, the
jury voted 8 to 4 for life without parole, but the judge over-
rode it. What Justice Sotomayor notes is that Alabama has
become an outlier, and that while in the 1980s and 1990s
there were a number of life sentences overridden by judges,
Alabama is the only state that continues to do so. Of the
twenty-seven life-to-death judge overrides in the 2000s, only
one *wasn't* from Alabama (it was in Delaware and was subsequently reversed for a life sentence). What explains this, asks
the justice? Her answer is politics:

The only answer that is supported by empirical evidence
is one that, in my view, casts a cloud of illegitimacy over
the criminal justice system: Alabama judges, who are
elected in partisan proceedings, appear to have suc-
cumbed to electoral pressures. . . . One Alabama judge,
who has overridden jury verdicts to impose the death
penalty on six occasions, campaigned by running several
advertisements voicing his support for capital punishment. One of these ads boasted that he had "presided
over more than 9,000 cases, including some of the most
heinous murder trials in our history," and expressly

named some of the defendants whom he had sentenced
to death, in at least one case over a jury's contrary judgment. . . . With admirable candor, another judge, who has
overridden one jury verdict to impose death, admitted
that voter reaction does "have some impact, especially in
high-profile cases." . . . "Let's face it," the judge said,
"we're human beings. I'm sure it affects some more than
others." (Citations omitted)[6]

What this dissent acknowledges is something that most
death penalty practitioners know somewhere in their souls;
there is something political to be gained by another's death.
Sometimes it is obvious; as in the re-election campaign examples. But in some ways it is much harder to see.

One of those thorny political issues is money. Most people
think that it costs a lot to house someone in prison for a long
time (and it does), so it would be cheaper to execute someone. That isn't true, assuming you agree that there should be
a trial and some standards of fairness associated with those
trials should be met. (It undoubtedly would be cheaper to
arrest someone and then shoot them.) And in our history,
that is how it was done when the act of execution was the
sole responsibility of the sovereign. Today, however, we at
least strive to ensure that people who face the death penalty
are afforded protections to ensure that they really deserve
the punishment—something that is undoubtedly costing
death penalty jurisdictions a considerable amount of money.

For example, a new study of the cost of the death penalty
in Colorado revealed that capital proceedings require six
times more days in court and take much longer to resolve

than life-without-parole (LWOP) cases. The study, published in the *University of Denver Criminal Law Review*, found that LWOP cases required an average of 24.5 days of in-court time, while the death-penalty cases required 147.6 days. The authors noted that selecting a jury in an LWOP case takes about a day and a half; in a capital case, jury selection averages 26 days. In measuring the comparative time it takes to go from charging a defendant to final sentencing, the study found that LWOP cases took an average of 526 days to complete; death cases took almost four calendar years longer —1,902 days. The study found that even when a death-penalty case ends in a plea agreement and a life sentence, the process takes a year and a half longer than an LWOP case with a trial.[7]

The length of proceedings and the expenses involved with them are political because how we spend our resources is always a political decision, often referred to in economic texts as the "guns or butter" debate. About a year ago, the death penalty was almost repealed in the state of California by popular vote (it was upheld 52 percent to 48 percent), and a large part of the support for abolishment of the death penalty came as a result of startling fiscal information: a study authored by Judge Arthur Alarcon and Professor Paula Mitchell (2011, updated 2012) concluded that the cost of the death penalty in California has totaled over $4 billion since 1978: $1.94 billion for pre-trial and trial costs, $925 million for automatic appeals and state habeas corpus petitions, $775 million for federal habeas corpus appeals, and $1 billion for the costs of incarceration. The authors calculated that, if the governor commuted the sentences of those remaining on death row to life without parole, it would result in an immediate savings of $170 million per year, with a savings of $5 billion over the next twenty years.

The idea that housing an offender for the rest of his life is actually cheaper than executing him is counterintuitive, and many jurors who have voted for death in a particular case say things like they didn't want to feed the defendant for the rest of his life.

THE ADVERSARY SYSTEM

There are many reasons to be proud of the adversary system—it provides real checks and balances on power. But there are some side effects that are less salubrious. I want to start with prosecutors.

Prosecutors face a unique dilemma, they serve two masters: their civic responsibility: which tells them to seek justice, to do what is right in a particular case; and their ego, which is responsible for their ambition and the ineffable desire to win—sometimes at all costs. We have certainly seen this play out with the so-called Brady rule in recent times. Under a United States Supreme Court case called *Brady v. Maryland*,[8] the prosecution is charged with turning over to the defense anything that is or could be exculpatory of the defendant either regarding his guilt or innocence or as to sentencing. An example of something exculpatory would be the failure of an eyewitness to identify the defendant in a line-up. Yet there are many times that exculpatory information is not turned over by the prosecution; for example, you will see how that happened in one of my cases which I discuss later in this book. Indeed, this inability to identify what is exculpatory, or willingness to ignore this duty, is a challenge of national proportions.[9]

Unfortunately, many prosecutors' offices only reward those who win cases—not only with advancement opportunities, but sometimes also monetary incentives. For example, in fall 2011, the American Bar Association (ABA) found that a district attorney in Colorado paid prosecutors bonuses for obtaining at least a 70 percent conviction rate in five or more felony trials in one year.[10] However, at the end of the day, some of the most dangerous incentives for prosecutors may be those that deal with political power. Cook County, Illinois, which includes the city of Chicago, is no stranger to the pressures of politics prosecutors face in deciding whether to charge or try specific cases. In 2013, Anita Alvarez, the Cook County State's Attorney, suspended two prosecutors after the press reported that the two prosecutors had decided not to bring charges against a man who later burned himself, his wife, and his daughter.[11] Later that year, another prosecutor resigned her position after she was suspended for dropping the charges against several young girls in juvenile court after realizing that the evidence against the girls was not strong and that the police's identification procedures were extremely suggestive and prone to inaccuracy.[12] These decisions suspending assistant state attorneys, according to the former prosecutor, leave the rest of the office "second-guessing their judgment" about the way they want to pursue their cases. These prosecutors were dismissed for violating the culture of their offices—for not being "tough"—but is it tough to prosecute those against whom you do not have solid evidence?

Although politics are involved in most prosecutions, they are especially evident in possible death penalty cases through the choices that prosecutors make. It is important to remember that the prosecution decides whether or not to ask for the death penalty, and that choice enormously impacts the way the trial will proceed.

In other words, once the prosecution makes the decision to ask for the death penalty, everything changes. Both sides must prepare for two trials—the trial of the case and the trial of the defendant's life. More experts must be engaged on both sides, motions practice ramps up—all of the matters I have discussed before. So how does that decision get made? There are a lot of factors that go into it, some of which one might expect: Does the case fall into a category of murder that allows for the death penalty? Is there strong evidence of guilt? Does the defendant have a bad and/or violent history? Questions like these are relatively objective, and one can follow them. But other matters enter into the decision that may not be as visible or salient. These are more subjective issues—things like how the defendant looks. By this I do mean race, but not just race—does he look "bad" enough to kill? How does one figure that out? Is the crime "bad enough"? These are matters where bias easily enters into the equation. Is there political pressure to ask for death? Not to?

Because of the extreme costs involved in pursuing a death sentence in a case, the government, whether federal or state, essentially makes an investment in seeking capital offenders' deaths when a prosecutor seeks the death penalty. The governmental investment includes the obvious monetary considerations. However, many death penalty cases also require a political investment into reaching a death sentence at almost all costs. Unfortunately, most of the pressure falls not onto the big players, such as the attorney general or the state prosecutor, but the individual prosecutors who do the legwork for them. Thus, although the conflicts prosecutors face between their desire to do the right thing, that is, "seek justice," and their desire to win the case for their own ego or personal gain can manifest in all cases, the death penalty's "high stakes" nature makes this conflict more readily apparent in death penalty cases.

As discussed in the previous chapter, even though a defendant technically has the right to trial by a jury of his or her peers, death penalty cases allow for the exclusion of jurors who stand against the death penalty and would not vote to impose it.[13] Moreover, as a matter of practice and strategy, in choosing a capital jury, many prosecutors seek to keep jurors who will be more predisposed to voting for the death penalty, which often results in a marked exclusion of black jurors—a practice that has been outlawed by the Supreme

Court as a violation of the Equal Protection Clause but nevertheless continues.[14] But why would prosecutors want to remove black jurors from serving in a capital jury? The answer to this question can actually encompass quite a number of things. First, as discussed in the previous chapter, there is a significant number of black capital defendants, and prosecutors might feel that black jurors are less likely to impose the death penalty on another member of the black community. One only needs to look at the literature following the infamous O. J. Simpson trial to see that people continue operating under an assumption that black jurors will not convict black defendants. Moreover, black jurors are, statistically speaking, likely to vote against and influence other jurors into voting against death based on a number of reasons, including their own experiences with the law and their religious convictions.[15] Race, and its larger role in politics, both historically and currently, will be discussed in more detail in the next section.

However, even when race is not necessarily a significant factor in jury selection, prosecutors nevertheless focus juror strikes on people they might fear are sympathetic to the defendant or generally rebellious (in fact, both were listed in the "Batson Justifications" document from the *Golphin* case that will be discussed below), effectively stacking the jury with people who are unlikely to have an open mind toward the defendant. The so-called death-qualification of juries further exacerbates the skewed nature of capital jurors—by weeding out people who are unsure or have reservations toward the death penalty or people who have had brushes with the criminal justice system as "undesirable" for a capital jury, jurors who remain may have a tainted idea of what their role in a capital jury is—to be a stamp on the prosecutor's decision to seek the death penalty.[16] Unsurprisingly, capital trials often become less about whether the defendant is guilty at all (even the Supreme Court has assumed that death-qualified juries are more prone to convicting a defendant than non-death-qualified juries), and more about whether the defendant will receive the death penalty or not.[17] Even more alarming is that mock jury scenarios have shown that many jurors assume that they are *supposed* to impose the death penalty and may sometimes shift the burden to the defendant to prove that he deserves to live.[18] Jurors' misguided understanding of their role in the penalty phase of a capital case can be seen through their reactions when they choose life over death. For example, after voting against imposing the death penalty in a media-sensational case, one juror told local news outlets that she felt like the jurors had "failed the system" even though there is nothing wrong with returning a life verdict.[19] A similar sentiment was expressed by other jurors in high-profile death penalty cases, including the Casey Anthony case after the jury not only took the death penalty off the table, but also acquitted her of the first-degree murder charge—a fact that was exploited by then-prosecutor Jeff Ashton when he ran against his boss to become the new Orange-Osceola County State Attorney the year following the Anthony trial.[20]

These instances and problems in the death penalty system—most of which are prosecutor-driven—thus invite the question: does the adversarial nature of the criminal justice system open the door to injustice in death penalty cases? Is there really any justice when a man gets a death verdict after weeding out the peers who may have been sympathetic to him?

RACE AND THE DEATH PENALTY

In many ways, the role of race in the death penalty is the most politically volatile aspect of capital punishment in the United States. Historically, especially in the South, a condemnation to death was used as a tool of oppression against young black boys and men—that condemnation manifested itself through vigilante acts, that is, lynching, that left thousands of black victims dead after the dawn of the Reconstruction Era.[21] Although lynchings in the South were not actually legal and were often carried out without authorization from the courts, the fact that various legal actors presided over lynchings and that perpetrators were seldom prosecuted for taking part in lynchings made them de facto government-sanctioned executions where the public served as judge, jury, and executioner. When integrated with the capital punishment institution, the pervasive use of the legal system as a racially motivated system in former lynching states, which continued targeting black men in alleged rapes against white women for the death penalty, led to a moratorium on the American death penalty. [22]

In 1972, the U.S. Supreme Court declared the moratorium on the death penalty after it found that the death penalty was impermissibly being imposed on the basis of the defendants' race. For example, in Texas, between 1924 and 1968, white defendants would often be sentenced to life in prison while black defendants were sentenced to death even though they were codefendants and had been convicted for the same crimes, albeit in different trials. [23] Moreover, although the death penalty was unusual for rape cases, many of the rape cases that resulted in a death sentence involved black defendants. Recognizing the undeniable role of race, the Court found that the imposition of the death penalty, under the circumstances at that time, would constitute cruel and unusual punishment in violation of the Eighth and Fourteenth Amendments. As Justice Stewart eloquently stated:

> These death sentences are cruel and unusual in the same way that being struck by lightning is cruel and unusual. For, of all the people convicted of rapes and murders in 1967 and 1968, many just as reprehensible as these, the petitioners are among a capriciously selected random handful upon whom the sentence of death has in fact been imposed. My concurring Brothers have demonstrated that, if any basis can be discerned for the selection of these few to be sentenced to die, it is the constitutionally impermissible basis of race. . . . [T]he Eighth and Fourteenth Amendments cannot tolerate the infliction of a sentence of death under legal systems that permit this

unique penalty to be so wantonly and so freakishly imposed.[24]

Although the administration of the death penalty seemingly no longer involves the serious or systemic imposition of the death penalty based on defendant race discrimination to the extent that led to its moratorium in 1972, racial bias in the charging and imposition of the death penalty continues to exist today. However, the racial bias that exists today revolves around the apparent devaluation of victims of color and the resulting higher rate of death penalty sentences for offenders who murder white victims. The Supreme Court, in the 1987 case *McCleskey v. Kemp*, was presented with evidence showing not only that there was noticeable leniency in cases involving black and Latino victims, but also that, in cases involving white victims and black defendants, black defendants were sentenced to death at an even higher rate.[25] It is important to note that McCleskey was presenting evidence of the racial bias in the administration of the Georgia death penalty. Georgia, which was a confederate state and had the last recorded lynching, the victims being two black married couples, in 1946, had a history of racial tension.[26] Nevertheless, the Supreme Court held that McCleskey did not show a violation of the Eighth or Fourteenth Amendments because he did not prove that the jurors had discriminatory intent. The Court refused to declare a second moratorium on the death penalty.

Thus, although the reinstatement of state death penalty schemes purported to ensure that the death penalty is no longer imposed based on the color of a defendant's skin, the color of a defendant's skin, as well as the victim's, continues to play a role in who lives and who dies. Since the reinstatement of the death penalty, cases involving interracial murders involving black offender and white victims are executed at thirteen times the rate of murders involving white offenders and black victims.[27] The devaluing of victims of color and the subsequent imposition of the death penalty on offenders who kill white victims is ultimately a moral and a political issue for several reasons. Because imposition of the death penalty is not permissible on the basis of the race of the offender or the victim, offenders who are sentenced to death based on the race of their victim are illegally sentenced to death. Moreover, on a more theoretical level, the acceptance of the devaluation of victims of color may be inadvertently sending the message to future offenders that killing people of color is more morally permissible than killing their white counterparts and is thus inconsistent with a desire for general deterrence. The imposition of the death penalty based on a victim's, and in some cases the defendant's, race rather than on the moral culpability of the offender based on his actions is also inconsistent with retributive justice because the disparate treatment between offenders is not based on their actions, but on an arbitrary valuation of victims based on the color of their skin.

This issue is also political because it shows that the U.S. justice system tends to pursue death sentences in cases involving "worthy" victims. Because a death penalty prosecution is long and difficult for prosecutors, they may want to ensure that they have something to gain from taking on these difficult and time-consuming cases. Unfortunately, that generally tends to mean discounting murders involving certain people, often of poor socioeconomic status and very often of color.[28] For example, even though the Los Angeles area has a well-known problem with gang-related murder (the Los Angeles Police Department attributed 105 homicides, or 60 percent of the total number of homicides for the L.A. area, to gangs or gang members in 2012), gang-related murders do not tend to involve the risk of the death penalty unless other circumstances are involved—these circumstances often manifest as either "innocent" victims who were not involved in gangs, juvenile victims, or offenders who have claimed multiple murder victims.[29]

Apart from the race of the victim and the defendant, race often comes into play with jury selection as well. As recently as 2012, in the case of *North Carolina v. Golphin et al.*, a North Carolina judge granted the defendants' motions to vacate their death sentences after review of the case showed that race was a significant factor for prosecutors in excluding black potential jurors at jury selection.[30] Specifically, the court considered the prosecutors' notes next to each black potential juror with notations such as "blk. wino—drugs," "thug," and "blk/high drug," while similar white potential jurors' notations included items such as "drinks—country boy—ok," or "ne'er do well," as well as the large statistical increase in likelihood of black jurors being struck in compar-

ison to their white counterparts.[31] The court also expressed
discomfort with the prosecutors' use of language from a
cheat-sheet, titled "Batson Justifications: Articulating Juror
Negatives," which was distributed to prosecutors, in explaining the juror strikes without having to mention their race.[32]

Perhaps the most dangerous factor in race and the death
penalty today is the idea that, having elected our first black
president, we are now living in a post-racial America. Unfortunately, even since President Obama took office, the statistics continue to look dim for offenders of color who kill white
victims. A look into racial statistics in the Texas death penalty
system up to 2011 (and accounting for all executions in the
state since 1976) showed that although Texas had executed
470 people, a third of the national total at the time, *only one
of those executions involved a white defendant and a black
victim.*[33]

REAL IMPLICATIONS FOR PRACTITIONERS

Naturally, the political and racial pressures involved in a
death penalty case can have a strain on a defendant's relationship with his or her attorney because, as previously discussed, death cases can shift the focus of whether the client
is guilty at all to whether he wants to take a chance with a
jury despite the various factors working against him. This
reality is especially difficult for abolitionist death penalty defense practitioners because, unfortunately, power over death
is still used as a political tool by politicians who value "law

and order" and can often be destructive to people who do not see the death penalty as an appropriate tool for maintenance of law and order. Thus, many death penalty defense attorneys who take cases all the way to trial are often demonized by the prosecution, the public, the victim's family, and the media when a death verdict is either not delivered or overturned. Moreover, political pressure and potential backlash from the community, which could cost a defense attorney his or her reputation in front of potential clients, judges, employers, or even constituents, also shows practitioners how these types of politics might affect potential appointed lawyers in death penalty cases.

Ultimately, a stance against the death penalty in specific cases, even when defense lawyers are not necessarily advocating an abolitionist stance against the death penalty in general, can have severe consequences on that lawyer's ability to secure endorsements or seek leadership roles in the future. A recent example is Debo Adegbile, a former NAACP lawyer who was part of a death penalty appeal for Mumia Abu-Jamal, a man convicted of killing a Philadelphia police officer. As a result of the appeal filed by Adegbile, the Third Circuit Court of Appeals vacated Abu-Jamal's death sentence after finding that imposition of it was unconstitutional because the jury instructions in Abu-Jamal's trial were confusing so that jurors did not understand that they could consider mitigating circumstances even if all twelve jurors were in disagreement about them.[34] Thus, the death sentence was vacated based on a constitutional deficiency.

On November 18, 2013, President Obama nominated Adegbile to head the Civil Rights Division of the Department of Justice. However, an ugly campaign was brought against Adegbile led by the Fraternal Order of Police, which accused him of defending a "thug" and the "country's most notorious cop-killer" by "turn[ing] the justice system on its head with unfounded and unproven allegations of racism"[35] (Abu-Jamal's appellate team had raised a *Batson* claim after the prosecution used ten out of fifteen peremptory challenges to remove black jurors, though the Court of Appeals held that it had been waived and that Abu-Jamal did not meet the required standard either way). Moreover, because Adegbile's nomination was released dangerously close to midterm elections, numerous Republican politicians joined the campaign against Adegbile and refused to support his confirmation for the position, all while numerous Democrats were afraid of supporting the nomination for fear of losing support from the law enforcement community.[36] Accordingly, Adegbile's confirmation was continually pushed back— not because of some sort of ethical or moral deficiency in his personal life, but because of his zealous advocacy for a client facing death in the face of a constitutional violation during his trial.

Unfortunately, Adegbile is not alone. Again and again in U.S. history, people in the political world, when running for governor or for re-election onto the judicial bench, have faced extreme criticism for their roles in either challenging or overturning a death sentence, presenting the ultimate paradox of the situation: how can we trust that defense attorneys will be zealous advocates for their clients when they have so much to lose from winning their death cases?

Adegbile's story is also illustrative of the discomfort and defensiveness that comes from allegations of racism at all stages of the criminal justice system. Even though Abu-Jamal's jury ended up with ten white jurors and two black jurors after the prosecution struck ten other black potential jurors, unless there is overt racism such as in *Golphin*, many courts and commentators generally overlook or do not give much weight to other signs of racism in capital cases. However, even when the allegations of racism are not supported by "smoking gun" evidence, it is important for defense advocates to raise the issues at all stages of the case—in order to preserve the issues for appeal and also to address them as needed before trial—regardless of how uncomfortable racial conversations with judges and prosecutors may become. This is especially important because, as discussed earlier in this chapter, racism in charging, jury selection, and jury deliberations can be a matter of life and death in a capital case.

Although dealing with the implications of political and racial issues can be extremely difficult and quite delicate, it's important to note that they come with the territory when defending capital cases. Thus, one of the most important ways to address some of the political and racial undertones of any capital trial is to read between the lines of each charged case—why is this case so important? What are the types of messages the prosecution is trying to send by charging the case as a death case? Once there are answers to those questions, the next step is to be creative in attacking the problem. Great advocacy may sometimes require extensive motion practice, but in other circumstances, it may just take something as simple as an original idea and a phone call.

One such instance came up several years ago when an Oklahoma lawyer from a small town was assigned his very first death penalty case by the court. Panicking due to the fact that his practice was mostly concentrated in probate (wills and trusts), he called me and explained that his case involved two lesbians who had driven into town and shot a bank teller while they committed a robbery. A camera caught the whole thing. Moreover, the teller who was shot was the mayor's wife. Needless to say, there was tremendous political pressure for a death verdict against the lawyer's client. I asked the lawyer to find out what new things the town needed, but could not afford, by going to their county board meeting. A few days later, he called and let me know that the town was in desperate need of a fire engine. I advised the lawyer to submit a budget for the costs of prosecuting his client for a death verdict to the board president. Along with that, the lawyer submitted an offer to the prosecution for his client to plead guilty in return for a life sentence, plus one additional detail: the money saved from dropping a capital prosecution could buy a new fire engine and a plaque honoring the mayor's late wife. The townspeople agreed.

At the end of the day, crime, money, and race are all only a few facets of the way the death penalty is intertwined with politics. However, the attorney's duty to her client must always supersede any regard for possible political consequences. After all, a client's life is in the balance.

5

THE FAILURE AND FATE OF CAPITAL PUNISHMENT

I was sitting in my office, back when I was the director of the Illinois Capital Resource Center (the agency that represented all of the death row inmates in Illinois on state post-conviction and federal habeas corpus), when I got a call from Julie Harmon. Julie and I had worked together in the Cook County Public Defender's office. She was a good lawyer, and tough as they came.

"Andrea? It's Julie Harmon." she said.

"Hey Julie, how are you?"

"Andrea, you know the worst thing that ever happened to me?" I knew. Her husband, Tim, had died very young, and as I understood it, partially as a result of a problem that they shared—alcohol. Not that Julie has this problem anymore.

"Yes. Tim's death."

"Well the second worst is what I am calling you about. He is a client of mine. His name is Madison Hobley. He is on death row, his appeal has been affirmed. I have represented a lot of people, and you know I never say this, but he is innocent. The case is coming to you now." I swallowed. I had known Julie a long time. She was a skeptic, unsentimental, and hard to put one over on.

"Julie, I had no idea. You must feel awful," I murmured in response.

"I know you work with panel lawyers, Andrea." That was true. Including myself we had four lawyers, four investigators, and four mitigation specialists. There were at that time over 160 people on Illinois' death row, so we served as a training and investigative backstop for appointed lawyers on 90 percent of our cases and did the other 10 percent in house. I tried to put together teams that worked, with the appropriate backup from our in-house people, including me. "You have to promise me . . ." her voice broke a little.

"Julie," I said, "I will work on the case myself."

What else could I do? Walk away? Thus began the saga of my and Kurt Feuer's (who at the time was a lawyer with Ross & Hardies) representation of Madison Hobley, who had been wrongfully convicted, tortured into a false confession, and become a victim of a scheme where his prosecutor lied about failing to turn over exculpatory evidence, evidence was planted at the crime scene, and leads to the real killer or killers were ignored by the police.[1]

It took us years to clear Madison Hobley's name. We spent hundreds of hours reinvestigating every aspect of the case, researching, writing, and submitting arguments to various courts. We had to go to the Illinois Supreme Court to even get a hearing on the new evidence.[2]

Madison Hobley's case represents everything that is wrong with the death penalty, and it is my hope that his case will shed light on why it is that we must (and I believe will ultimately) abolish this practice in the United States.

To understand how nearly all of the ills of death penalty cases coalesced in this case, I am going to take some time to talk about what happened: the crime, the false and forced confession, the corrupt trial, the jury misconduct, and a bit about my former client, Madison Hobley, who, at the time of his arrest, was married with an infant son, was employed as a medical device installer, and had no prior criminal convictions. Madison Hobley was convicted of and sentenced to die for a January 1987 arson murder in which seven people, including his wife and infant son, died. Before I became involved in his case, his conviction and death sentence were affirmed on direct appeal.[3] He had also filed an amended post-conviction petition that was dismissed in July 1996.[4]

As Julie had told me, and as our reinvestigation of the case revealed, Madison was innocent. Here is what happened that fateful night:

On January 6, 1987, at approximately 2:00 a.m., Mr. Hobley awoke to the sound of a fire alarm in his building. He went out into the hall to investigate, leaving his wife and son in their apartment, apartment 301. His apartment was on the top floor of the building, at the end of the hallway and diagonally across the hall from the building's wooden stairwell.

Mr. Hobley thought that he saw some smoke coming from down the hall, and he walked in that direction, passing by the door to the building stairway. Fire was shooting out of the stairwell door, across the hallway, and into the opposite wall. He heard a popping sound behind him, and the hallway quickly began to fill with smoke blocking the way back to his apartment. Mr. Hobley could not physically get back to his apartment through the incredible heat, fire, and smoke, so he shouted to his wife to take their son and go to the window.

He then crawled out the back stairs and went to the alley behind the building in a pair of shorts and a T-shirt that he had been sleeping in. He had no shoes, pants, or coat.

While outside, Mr. Hobley helped save a baby by catching him from a second floor window. His wife and infant son did not make it out of the apartment and were ultimately overcome by smoke and died.

So how was it that he was convicted? The police tortured Mr. Hobley to elicit a confession.

The police officers investigating this arson became suspicious of Mr. Hobley when they learned that he had managed to escape the fire while his wife and son perished. The erroneous belief of these officers that Mr. Hobley would have either rescued his wife and son or perished in the fire himself led them to immediately focus on Mr. Hobley as the sole suspect and to drop any further investigative leads of other suspects. The physical evidence, however, convincingly shows that it would have been humanly impossible to pass through the wall of fire that blocked return to Mr. Hobley's apartment.

Worse yet, Mr. Hobley had the misfortune of falling into the hands of officers at Area Two under the command of known-torturer Jon Burge, officers who have been implicated in numerous other incidents of torture—so many that a torture commission has been created by the Illinois legislature to look into them.[5] These officers beat and "bagged" Mr. Hobley within hours of taking him into custody in a failed attempt to extract a "confession" from him. "Bagging" was the practice of Commander Burge and his self-described "ass-kickers" of placing a plastic typewriter cover over a suspect's face and head until the suspect lost consciousness due to lack of oxygen. Despite the seemingly improbable nature of this practice, the Chicago Police Department's Office of Professional Standards reported finding that this torture technique occurred at Area Two over at least a ten-year period, noting that a number of suspects with no opportunity to communicate with each other beforehand described being subjected to it.

The only existing police notes of Mr. Hobley's interrogation stated that Mr. Hobley denied involvement in the arson. One of his interrogators, Detective Dwyer, testified at trial that he did have notes of the confession, but that they got wet and were "a mess," so he threw them away. Officer Dwyer further testified at trial that Mr. Hobley confessed to the crime and that he told them he used a gas can that he threw down the second floor hallway after he set the fire.

The interrogating officers sent a third officer to the fire scene some fourteen hours after police and fire department investigators first entered the building. This officer recovered a gas can from the second floor of the building and that can showed no signs of having been in a fire. Since the physical evidence proved the gas can was not on the second floor hallway of the building *during* the fire, then Officer Dwyer's testimony about a confession to that fact had to be (and was) false.

The phony confession and the planted gas can were the primary pieces of evidence against Mr. Hobley at trial. In addition, the prosecution presented phony "physical" evidence about where the fire started—which Kurt and I, through our investigation, found to be conclusively false. Likewise, Bomb and Arson detective Virgil Mikus testified at trial that there was evidence that a pool of gasoline had been poured in the hallway in front of Mr. Hobley's apartment door and the fire ignited at that point. Yet once we had a real forensic review of the evidence, it was clear that did not happen.

At the post-conviction hearing where we exposed this falsehood, even the state's own expert, Dr. John DeHaan, testified that there was no physical evidence of a pool of gas having been poured in front of Mr. Hobley's apartment or of a particular point of ignition. Moreover, Detective Mikus, in his initial report, stated that he believed the fire started at the first-floor landing of the building stairwell, not in front of Mr. Hobley's apartment. This finding is consistent with that of Mr. Hobley's expert at the post-conviction hearing, Dr. Russell Ogle of Packer Engineering, Inc., in Naperville, Illinois.

In the state's case against Mr. Hobley, there also were two witnesses who (sort of) identified him as having bought a dollar's worth of gas for a one-gallon can the night of the fire although the container introduced at trial was a two-gallon can. I prefaced with "sort of" because only Andre Council positively identified Mr. Hobley, and he came forward only after seeing Mr. Hobley's arrest and "perp walk" broadcast on TV. And interestingly, Mr. Council has a lengthy arrest record, including an arrest for arson shortly after this fire, in the same neighborhood as Mr. Hobley's building, in which gasoline was ignited in a stairwell. This arrest and others, however, occurred while Council was a state's witness against Mr. Hobley, and Council was not prosecuted for any of his arrests until after Mr. Hobley's trial. In addition, Council received special treatment, including the waiver of a fingerprint check and the issuance of an I-Bond (allowing Council to leave custody without having to pay any money), pursuant to orders from Commander Burge, who directly intervened in at least some of Council's arrests during the pendency of Mr. Hobley's case, something that even trial prosecutor George Velcich admitted was highly unusual. Detective McWeeney, one of the officers who interrogated Mr. Hobley, also accompanied Mr. Council to court for one of his arrests and spoke to the person whom he believed to be the prosecutor about the case. That case was then dismissed.

The other identification regarding a gas can was uncertain, and came from Kenneth Stewart, who told us that the Chicago police pressured and threatened him to make an identification.[6]

The prosecution's "motive" evidence was speculative: Mr. Hobley had an extramarital affair. Mr. Hobley, however, had not only broken off the affair before the subject fire, but had told his wife and her family about it and asked for their forgiveness.

Moreover, the gas can that was introduced as corroboration of the confession was planted by the police at the scene. How do we know? A photograph of the gas can in the location at the fire scene shows where it was "found after" 5:00 p.m. on the day of the fire. However, the fire was sufficiently extinguished by around 3:00 a.m. that fire investigators were able to enter the building at that time, some fourteen hours earlier. Despite three searches by the responding firefighters and police before 5:00 p.m., they all missed a bright red gas can. The photograph, which was entered into evidence, shows the floor of apartment 206 where it was "found," the gas can, an open door (broken by the forced entry of a firefighter), and the floor of the hallway outside. The doorway depicted is the kitchen doorway to apartment 206, which the tenant testified at trial was never used and always locked. While there is some white material on the floor of apartment 206 (gypsum or plaster tracked in by a firefighter), the floor inside the apartment was significantly cleaner than the hallway floor just outside of the apartment, where a great deal of debris covers the hallway floor. This photograph clearly shows a straight line of demarcation across the doorway between the relatively clean inside apartment floor and the debris-covered hallway floor outside.

Each of the expert witnesses who testified at Mr. Hobley's post-conviction hearing—Dr. DeHaan and former fire chief Pat Burns, on behalf of the state, and Dr. Ogle on behalf of Mr. Hobley—agreed that this straight line of debris piled up in the hallway could only have occurred while the kitchen door was still closed. Otherwise the debris would have piled up inside the apartment as well, and it would not have been in a straight line of demarcation across the doorway where the locked door was.

While the kitchen door was still closed, it necessarily follows that the gas can would have had to be in the hallway outside of the kitchen door, and could not have been accidentally kicked or knocked into the apartment (as police witnesses surmised at trial) until after a firefighter broke down the kitchen door, opening the doorway. It therefore also necessarily follows that the gas can would have been subjected to being covered with the same amount of debris and material shown to have accumulated in the hallway along the kitchen doorway of apartment 206. The photo, however, clearly shows that the gas can is completely clean and free of the debris that is piled up along the doorway and in the hallway just outside of the apartment.

Thus, the state's position was that despite three waves of firefighters searching each apartment and numerous fire de-

partment and police department investigators having
combed the premises as part of the fire cause and origin
investigation, no one saw this bright red and yellow can for
some fourteen hours; there was still liquid gasoline in the can
despite the highly volatile nature of the liquid and the extreme temperatures present in the second-floor hallway
down to at least ankle-level above the floor.

Even given these circumstances, the small plastic vent cap
on the can was completely unmelted and free of soot despite
the high temperature and dense smoke in the hallway. Further, the red plastic child's chair shown next to the gas can
shows deformation due to heat, even though this chair was
never in the hallway during the fire and is farther from the
open door than the gas can. The gas can could not have been
in the hallway outside of apartment 206 during the fire.

After the filing of Mr. Hobley's first post-conviction petition, investigator Lee Smith, now a Chicago police officer,
telephoned the Evidence and Recovered Property Section
("ERPS") of the Chicago Police Department to follow up on
a subpoena requesting, among other things, the gas can used
to convict Mr. Hobley.

To his surprise, the individual with whom he spoke told
him that there was a second gas can associated with Mr.
Hobley's case, and gave him the inventory report number for
that can. This individual, believed to be Lavergne Drobitsch,
told Mr. Smith that she would send him a copy of the report.

A short time later, a supervisor at ERPS, Otto Marks,
telephoned Mr. Smith and told him that the second can

would not be produced without a court order. Shortly there-
after, Judge Porter dismissed Mr. Hobley's post-conviction
petition without requiring the state to even answer it and
without ordering the production of the can.

At argument before the Illinois Supreme Court on Mr.
Hobley's appeal of Judge Porter's ruling, the Court asked the
state for an explanation of what the second can concerned,
and the assistant state's attorney professed complete ignor-
ance about the contents of the report. In its opinion remand-
ing the case to Judge Porter for an evidentiary hearing, the
Illinois Supreme Court ordered the state to produce the second can.

While the state was tellingly obdurate in its persistent
refusal to produce the report or reveal its contents, once the
state was forced to divulge the report it adopted a very blasé
attitude, taking the position with Judge Porter that it concerned a completely different case and that Mr. Hobley's
counsel had been making a big deal about nothing.

A review of the report, however, revealed an astonishing
number of coincidences: The report inventoried a red and
yellow two-gallon gas can with a long, flexible metal spout,
just like the can used to convict Mr. Hobley; the officer who
inventoried the can was none other than Detective Virgil
Mikus, the same Bomb and Arson detective who investigated
Mr. Hobley's case and testified at trial against him; and the
can was used in an arson some three weeks before the arson
for which Mr. Hobley was convicted.

A review of ERPS's inventory ledger revealed a further intriguing fact: all of the several items pertaining to this earlier arson had been destroyed years earlier as part of ERPS's evidence destruction schedule save one—the gas can. ERPS's inventory ledger further revealed that this gas can was purportedly destroyed much later—only after Mr. Hobley issued his post-conviction subpoenas for further evidence.

An investigator for Mr. Hobley then tracked down the individual charged with that earlier arson, Donnell McKinley, in Michigan and showed him photos of the gas can used to convict Mr. Hobley. Mr. McKinley identified the gas can as the gas can he used in his arson. At the evidentiary hearing conducted pursuant to the Supreme Court's remand, Mr. McKinley was shown the actual gas can and unequivocally identified it as his. He stated that the long, flexible spout was attached because he and a friend used the can to fill a lawn mower they used for a summer lawn-cutting business. When questioned by the state about a peculiar dent in the narrow side of the can, Mr. McKinley without hesitation placed the bottom of the palm of his hand into the dent and convincingly demonstrated how he pressed into the can to squeeze the gas out of it when he committed his arson.

During Mr. Hobley's trial, Officer Paladino, who recovered the gas can, testified that the black smudges on the gas can were not soot from the fire, but fingerprint powder. Julie Harmon, after hearing this testimony, moved for a mistrial on the grounds that no fingerprint report had been turned over to the defense. In response to the defense motion, lead prosecutor Paul Tsukuno told the trial judge that no fingerprint report existed. This was a lie. Because the negative report had been written on a transmittal receipt (the report showed that there were no fingerprints suitable for comparison) instead of a more formal document, the prosecutor said he did not have to turn it over because it was not technically a report. Yet at trial time he said, affirmatively, there was no report.

Trial prosecutor George Velcich admitted at his deposition in the post-conviction proceedings that the gas can used to convict Mr. Hobley was not in fact used in the subject fire and that the can used to start the subject fire was never found. But when he took the stand at the post-conviction evidentiary hearing, Mr. Velcich testified that his deposition testimony was incorrect because he did not remember why he used the gas can at trial, and that perhaps he presented the gas can as evidence that might even be helpful to Mr. Hobley.

Mr. Velcich argued strongly at trial that the gas can corroborated the confession. He also argued at the eligibility phase of the trial that "Mr. Hobley chose not to leave his fingerprints on that can."

The physical evidence, the documentary evidence from ERPS, and the prevarications of the trial prosecutors all clearly and consistently show that the gas can used to convict Mr. Hobley was phony, planted evidence. The only thing that does not make sense in this entire case is the state's story that Mr. Hobley committed this crime and confessed to it.

Madison Hobley's case is an example of what goes wrong in capital cases—the court system repeatedly failed to do justice. In fact, the criminal system never did do justice for Mr. Hobley—it was former Illinois governor George Ryan.[7]

This is a complicated story of wrongful conviction, though my account is missing other components from this case, including, for example, threats made in the jury room to get holdouts to convict (the jury was out for four days on the question of guilt).

It is this story and the countless others like it that have caused many states to abolish the death penalty. It is the prospect of executing an *innocent person* that has given many pause. There are many reasons why the death penalty's days likely are numbered, but Madison Hobley's story takes us through many of them; the death-qualified jury wasn't sure he did it, but once pushed into a guilty verdict, voted to kill him (as we found out from juror interviews) because they thought they had to. Juries are more likely to get it wrong when they are politically homogeneous than when they have many points of view.[8]

The pressure to solve a capital case—especially one like Mr. Hobley's where seven people died—causes the police to go for the "solve" and then push facts around to make it work. The feeling that the jury had that if they convicted they had to kill the defendant, the corruption of the police and at least one of the prosecutors, and the unwillingness of

the system to look at itself and admit to a possible error—
these are the hallmarks of capital prosecutions.

Back in the early 1990s, I was the head of the Capital
Resource Center. An infamous serial killer named John
Wayne Gacy was set to be the first involuntary execution in
Illinois, but we did not represent Gacy as his case had pre-
dated the existence of the agency. While there were two
black death row inmates whose cases had been final longer
than Gacy's, the powers that be put Gacy's execution first on
the list. It made it much harder to protest executions when
the first execution was of a man who had seduced and murdered thirty-three young men, buried them under his house,
and was white to boot.

Because this was the first person set for execution, a debate was held at Kent Law School about the death penalty. I
was one of the debaters, as were two prosecutors and a
member of the clergy. I had been at the resource center
about three years at this point and we had begun to discover
just how many death row inmates with affirmed death sentences were the wrong guy altogether. During part of my
remarks, I said that I had been surprised and horrified to
discover that about 10 to 15 percent of the men on death row
were the wrong guy altogether—a statistic that came from
our findings after we reinvestigated the death row cases. At
the time, I had the sense that the audience might not have
credited my statement, but now we know my estimate was
correct; we have executed twelve men in Illinois and exonerated nineteen from death row.

As I made that statement, William Kunkle, who had been the lead prosecutor of Gacy, interrupted me. "On no no no," he said. "That number is all wrong. The error rate is more like 5 percent or a bit less. And that," he said, "is an acceptable margin of error." I turned to him and told him he felt that way because he knew that this "acceptable margin of error" was not ever going to be him or anyone who was from his socioeconomic background—a statement he did not bother denying. However, we have to remember that the bell tolls for us all.

I have been asked to debate the death penalty many times during my career, and I have found that the reasons people really support the death penalty are usually less obvious and more insidious than the ones mentioned in debates. Even as it sometimes works for justice, the media often adds support and hype for the death penalty. And frequently, the death penalty is a political matter for prosecutors and politicians who are rewarded for being tough on crime. However, the most encompassing justification of the death penalty comes down to retribution. Put another way, many people feel that some people just shouldn't be on this earth, that what they did was just too awful. The desire for retribution is a powerful one, and trying to deny someone the "right" to feel that way is foolish.

People feel what they feel, and if someone feels that certain crimes just "deserve" death, no amount of exhortations to the contrary will change those feelings. Today, support for and use of the death penalty are already declining. The polit-

ical realities of our economic situation and the growing rec-
ognition that our "war" on crime has boomeranged mean
that the death penalty's days are numbered.

Here is what I also know—most people don't know these
defendants intimately. They don't know their life stories,
what circumstances drove them to be where they were and
now are, and can't see their humanity until it's placed before
them in a sentencing hearing—if they are lucky enough to
see a sentencing hearing done by someone competent who
cares.

It's a selective blindness that we develop—we can't ab-
sorb all the pain around us, so we just don't look. We don't
see the homeless man we pass by, or the mentally ill woman
who is talking wildly to herself, or the children going to
school day after day in the same clothes where they will eat
their only meal, the free school lunch. I am not saying that
this blindness, this choice not to see the truth, makes us bad,
or inhumane—we have to defend ourselves from overload or
we can't do anyone any good. But while no one can do everything, everyone can do *something*.

I have chosen to try to tell my clients' stories, to help
other lawyers tell their clients' stories, and to teach my students of the value of each of our clients' lives. I have represented gang members, a serial rapist-murderer, several para-
noid schizophrenics, battered and abused women, and battered and abused men. Their stories are shocking, desperate-
ly moving and occasionally, in spite of everything, downright
funny. Some, indeed, committed the acts they were accused

of, and some did not. But no matter what they did or did not do, I believe that every person I have defended is a human being of value. Some are terribly damaged; some lack even tenuous connections with reality. Each of their lives tells us about the ways in which individuals and institutions can go horribly astray, but they also reveal what remains human and noble in the midst of such waste.

We are, and must remain, a nation of laws—not of the mob. The death penalty does not make us safer; we convict and execute wrongly and we spend precious resources on a system that doesn't work and never can.

APPENDIX A: DEATH PENALTY HISTORICAL TIMELINE

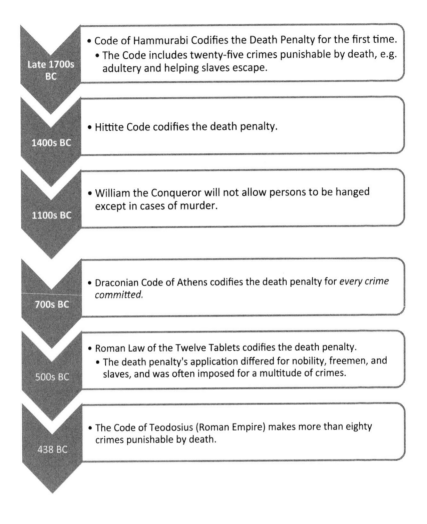

Late 1700s BC
- Code of Hammurabi Codifies the Death Penalty for the first time.
  - The Code includes twenty-five crimes punishable by death, e.g. adultery and helping slaves escape.

1400s BC
- Hittite Code codifies the death penalty.

1100s BC
- William the Conqueror will not allow persons to be hanged except in cases of murder.

700s BC
- Draconian Code of Athens codifies the death penalty for *every crime committed.*

500s BC
- Roman Law of the Twelve Tablets codifies the death penalty.
  - The death penalty's application differed for nobility, freemen, and slaves, and was often imposed for a multitude of crimes.

438 BC
- The Code of Teodosius (Roman Empire) makes more than eighty crimes punishable by death.

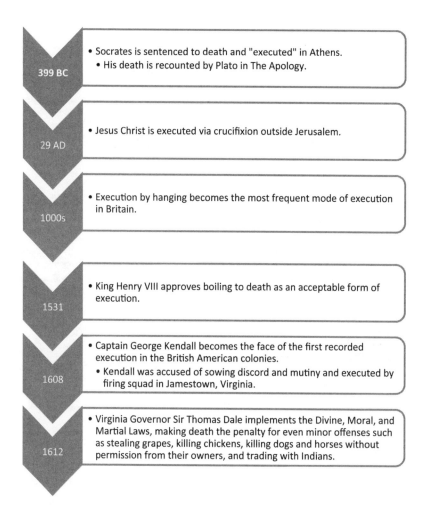

399 BC
- Socrates is sentenced to death and "executed" in Athens.
  - His death is recounted by Plato in The Apology.

29 AD
- Jesus Christ is executed via crucifixion outside Jerusalem.

1000s
- Execution by hanging becomes the most frequent mode of execution in Britain.

1531
- King Henry VIII approves boiling to death as an acceptable form of execution.

1608
- Captain George Kendall becomes the face of the first recorded execution in the British American colonies.
  - Kendall was accused of sowing discord and mutiny and executed by firing squad in Jamestown, Virginia.

1612
- Virginia Governor Sir Thomas Dale implements the Divine, Moral, and Martial Laws, making death the penalty for even minor offenses such as stealing grapes, killing chickens, killing dogs and horses without permission from their owners, and trading with Indians.

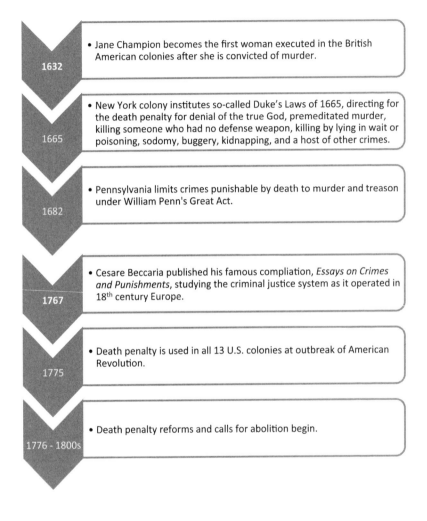

1632
- Jane Champion becomes the first woman executed in the British American colonies after she is convicted of murder.

1665
- New York colony institutes so-called Duke's Laws of 1665, directing for the death penalty for denial of the true God, premeditated murder, killing someone who had no defense weapon, killing by lying in wait or poisoning, sodomy, buggery, kidnapping, and a host of other crimes.

1682
- Pennsylvania limits crimes punishable by death to murder and treason under William Penn's Great Act.

1767
- Cesare Beccaria published his famous compliation, *Essays on Crimes and Punishments*, studying the criminal justice system as it operated in 18th century Europe.

1775
- Death penalty is used in all 13 U.S. colonies at outbreak of American Revolution.

1776 - 1800s
- Death penalty reforms and calls for abolition begin.

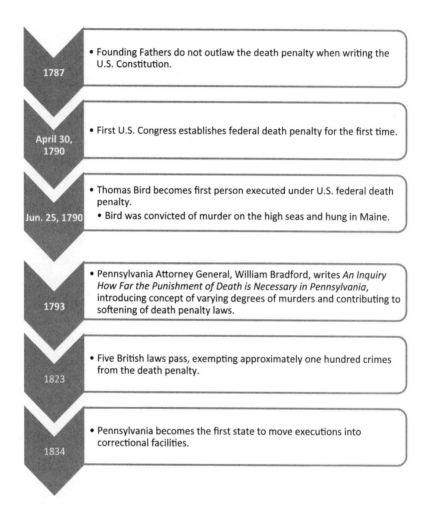

1787
- Founding Fathers do not outlaw the death penalty when writing the U.S. Constitution.

April 30, 1790
- First U.S. Congress establishes federal death penalty for the first time.

Jun. 25, 1790
- Thomas Bird becomes first person executed under U.S. federal death penalty.
- Bird was convicted of murder on the high seas and hung in Maine.

1793
- Pennsylvania Attorney General, William Bradford, writes *An Inquiry How Far the Punishment of Death is Necessary in Pennsylvania*, introducing concept of varying degrees of murders and contributing to softening of death penalty laws.

1823
- Five British laws pass, exempting approximately one hundred crimes from the death penalty.

1834
- Pennsylvania becomes the first state to move executions into correctional facilities.

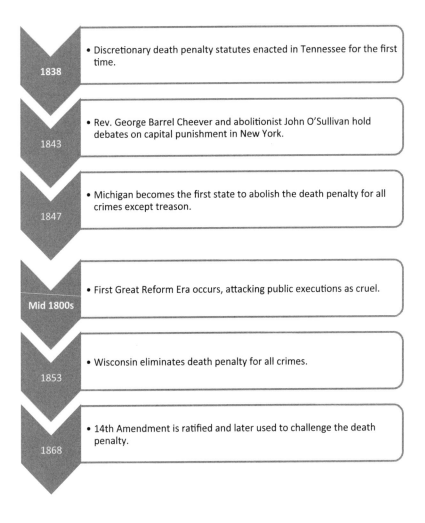

1838
- Discretionary death penalty statutes enacted in Tennessee for the first time.

1843
- Rev. George Barrel Cheever and abolitionist John O'Sullivan hold debates on capital punishment in New York.

1847
- Michigan becomes the first state to abolish the death penalty for all crimes except treason.

Mid 1800s
- First Great Reform Era occurs, attacking public executions as cruel.

1853
- Wisconsin eliminates death penalty for all crimes.

1868
- 14th Amendment is ratified and later used to challenge the death penalty.

Aug. 6, 1890
- William Kemmler becomes the first person executed by electrocution after he is convicted of murdering his mistress with an ax.
- Kemmler was executed via two applications of electricity and burst into flames after four minutes of the second charge-- 2,000 volts.

1895-1917
- Nine states abolish capital punishment and Congress reduces the number of federal capital crimes from approximately sixty to only three nonmilitary offenses (treason, murder, and rape) during Second Great Reform Era.

May 2, 1910
- U.S. Supreme Court decides *Weems v. United States*, the first major case tying crimes and proportionality of punishment together (and striking down the punishment for a Philippine law criminalizing the falsifying of a public/official document).

1910-1920
- Washington, Arizona, and Oregon reinstate the death penalty.

1924
- The use of cyanide gas introduced as a more humane execution method than electrocution.
  - The first person to be executed this way was Gee Jon, a Chinese immigrant who was convicted of murdering a rival gang member.

1930
- Eva Dugan's botched hanging in Arizona leads to public discourse pressuring more states to convert to more "civilized" methods of execution.

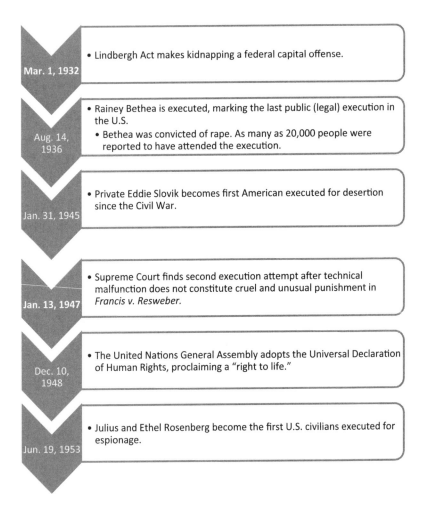

Mar. 1, 1932
- Lindbergh Act makes kidnapping a federal capital offense.

Aug. 14, 1936
- Rainey Bethea is executed, marking the last public (legal) execution in the U.S.
  - Bethea was convicted of rape. As many as 20,000 people were reported to have attended the execution.

Jan. 31, 1945
- Private Eddie Slovik becomes first American executed for desertion since the Civil War.

Jan. 13, 1947
- Supreme Court finds second execution attempt after technical malfunction does not constitute cruel and unusual punishment in *Francis v. Resweber.*

Dec. 10, 1948
- The United Nations General Assembly adopts the Universal Declaration of Human Rights, proclaiming a "right to life."

Jun. 19, 1953
- Julius and Ethel Rosenberg become the first U.S. civilians executed for espionage.

1957-1972

- Several states, including Michigan, Oregon, Iowa, New York, West Virginia, Vermont, and New Mexico, abolish death penalty after England and Canada produce exhaustive studies criticizing the death penalty.

Mar. 31, 1958

- U.S. Supreme Court, in *Trop v. Dulles*, rules that the Eighth Amendment requires that the state's power to punish is exercised within the limits of civilized standards of decency.

Jun. 3, 1968

- U.S. Supreme Court, in *Witherspoon v. Illinois*, holds that potential jurors who simply oppose the death penalty as a matter of personal belief, but who will still consider imposing it as instructed, cannot be dismissed for cause.

Jun. 29, 1972

- U.S. Supreme Court, in *Furman v. Georgia*, rules the death penalty unconstitutional as administered throughout the states and overturns over 600 death sentences.

Nov. 21, 1974

- United States Conference of Catholic Bishops publicly opposes the death penalty.

1976

- Portugal abolishes the death penalty for all crimes.

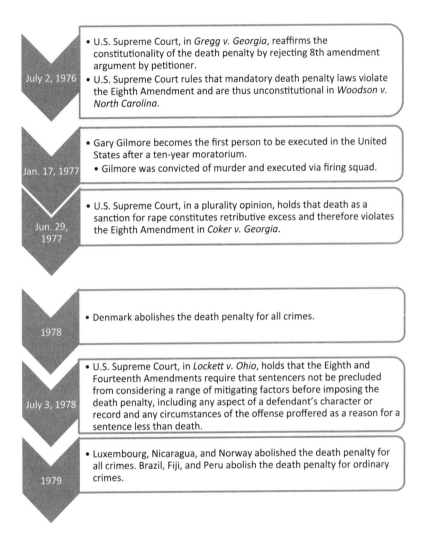

July 2, 1976
- U.S. Supreme Court, in *Gregg v. Georgia*, reaffirms the constitutionality of the death penalty by rejecting 8th amendment argument by petitioner.
- U.S. Supreme Court rules that mandatory death penalty laws violate the Eighth Amendment and are thus unconstitutional in *Woodson v. North Carolina*.

Jan. 17, 1977
- Gary Gilmore becomes the first person to be executed in the United States after a ten-year moratorium.
- Gilmore was convicted of murder and executed via firing squad.

Jun. 29, 1977
- U.S. Supreme Court, in a plurality opinion, holds that death as a sanction for rape constitutes retributive excess and therefore violates the Eighth Amendment in *Coker v. Georgia*.

1978
- Denmark abolishes the death penalty for all crimes.

July 3, 1978
- U.S. Supreme Court, in *Lockett v. Ohio*, holds that the Eighth and Fourteenth Amendments require that sentencers not be precluded from considering a range of mitigating factors before imposing the death penalty, including any aspect of a defendant's character or record and any circumstances of the offense proffered as a reason for a sentence less than death.

1979
- Luxembourg, Nicaragua, and Norway abolished the death penalty for all crimes. Brazil, Fiji, and Peru abolish the death penalty for ordinary crimes.

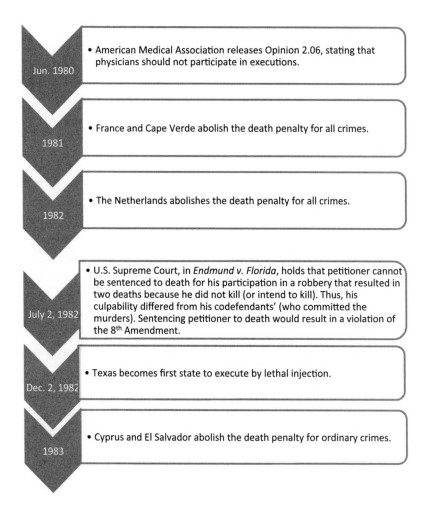

Jun. 1980
- American Medical Association releases Opinion 2.06, stating that physicians should not participate in executions.

1981
- France and Cape Verde abolish the death penalty for all crimes.

1982
- The Netherlands abolishes the death penalty for all crimes.

July 2, 1982
- U.S. Supreme Court, in *Endmund v. Florida*, holds that petitioner cannot be sentenced to death for his participation in a robbery that resulted in two deaths because he did not kill (or intend to kill). Thus, his culpability differed from his codefendants' (who committed the murders). Sentencing petitioner to death would result in a violation of the 8th Amendment.

Dec. 2, 1982
- Texas becomes first state to execute by lethal injection.

1983
- Cyprus and El Salvador abolish the death penalty for ordinary crimes.

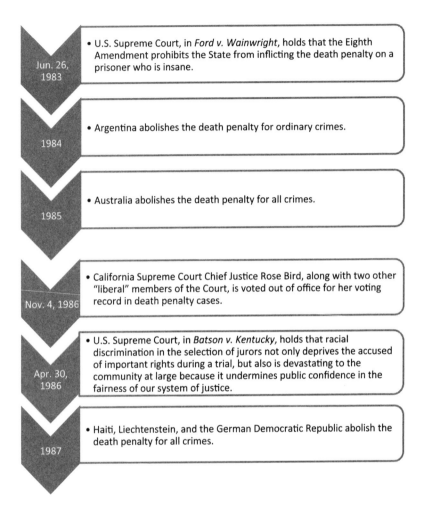

Jun. 26, 1983 — • U.S. Supreme Court, in *Ford v. Wainwright*, holds that the Eighth Amendment prohibits the State from inflicting the death penalty on a prisoner who is insane.

1984 — • Argentina abolishes the death penalty for ordinary crimes.

1985 — • Australia abolishes the death penalty for all crimes.

Nov. 4, 1986 — • California Supreme Court Chief Justice Rose Bird, along with two other "liberal" members of the Court, is voted out of office for her voting record in death penalty cases.

Apr. 30, 1986 — • U.S. Supreme Court, in *Batson v. Kentucky*, holds that racial discrimination in the selection of jurors not only deprives the accused of important rights during a trial, but also is devastating to the community at large because it undermines public confidence in the fairness of our system of justice.

1987 — • Haiti, Liechtenstein, and the German Democratic Republic abolish the death penalty for all crimes.

Apr. 22, 1987

- U.S. Supreme Court, in *McCleskey v. Kemp*, rejects the claim that death penalty sentencing in Georgia was administered with purposeful discrimination (and with discriminatory effect) in violation of the Eighth and Fourteenth Amendments despite statistical data on capital sentences in Georgia showing that black defendants who were convicted of killing white victims were more likely to be given the death sentence than other defendants.

Nov. 1987

- Hugo Adam Bedau and Michael L. Radelet publish *Miscarriages of Justice in Potentially Capital Cases*, documenting 350 twentieth-century cases of a wrongful conviction in potentially capital cases (and 23 cases involving the execution of an innocent person).

Jun. 29, 1988

- U.S. Supreme Court, in *Thompson v. Oklahoma*, rules that the execution of a person who was under 16 at the time of the offense violates the Eighth Amendment's prohibition against cruel and unusual punishments applied to the states through the Fourteenth Amendment.

1989

- Cambodia, New Zealand, Romania, and Slovenia abolish the death penalty for all crimes.

Jun. 26, 1989

- U.S. Supreme Court, in *Penry v. Lynaugh*, rules that the Eighth Amendment does not categorically prohibit the execution of mentally retarded capital murderers.

1990

- Andorra, Croatia, the Czech and Slovak Federal Republic, Hungary, Ireland, Mozambique, Nambia, and Sao Tome and Principle abolished the death penalty for all crimes.

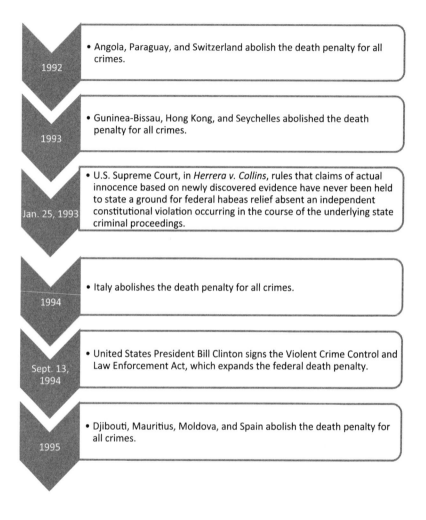

1992
- Angola, Paraguay, and Switzerland abolish the death penalty for all crimes.

1993
- Guninea-Bissau, Hong Kong, and Seychelles abolished the death penalty for all crimes.

Jan. 25, 1993
- U.S. Supreme Court, in *Herrera v. Collins*, rules that claims of actual innocence based on newly discovered evidence have never been held to state a ground for federal habeas relief absent an independent constitutional violation occurring in the course of the underlying state criminal proceedings.

1994
- Italy abolishes the death penalty for all crimes.

Sept. 13, 1994
- United States President Bill Clinton signs the Violent Crime Control and Law Enforcement Act, which expands the federal death penalty.

1995
- Djibouti, Mauritius, Moldova, and Spain abolish the death penalty for all crimes.

1996
- Belgium abolishes the death penalty for all crimes.

Apr. 24, 1996
- U.S. President Bill Clinton signs the Anti-Terrorism and Effective Death Penalty Act, restricting review in federal courts.

1997
- Georgia, Nepal, Poland, and South Africa abolish the death penalty for all crimes
- Bolivia abolishes the death penalty for ordinary crimes.

Feb. 3, 1997
- American Bar Association urges a halt to executions until each jurisdiction that imposes the death penalty eliminates any flaws in the system under which the penalty is imposed and carried out.

1998
- Azerbaijan, Bulgaria, Canada, Estonia, Lithuania, and the United Kingdom abolish the death penalty for all crimes.

Feb. 3, 1998
- Karla Faye Tucker, convicted murderer of two, is executed in Texas, provoking international dissent.

Mar. 31, 1998
- Judy Buenoano, the so-called "Black Widow," becomes the first woman executed in Florida in 150 years.
  - Buenoano was executed via electric chair.

Nov. 1998
- Northwestern University holds the first National Conference on Wrongful Convictions and the Death Penalty.

1999
- East Timor, Turkmenistan, and the Ukraine abolish the death penalty for all crimes.
  - Latvia abolishes the death penalty for ordinary crimes.

Jan. 27, 1999
- Pope John Paul II visits St. Louis, Missouri, and calls for the end to the death penalty.

Mar. 3, 1999
- Arizona executes Walter LaGrand in the last gas chamber execution to date.
  - LaGrand, a German national, died after eighteen minutes in the gas chamber.

April 1999
- U.N. Human Rights Commission adopts Resolution 1999/61, supporting a worldwide moratorium on executions.

June 1999
- Russian President Boris Yeltsin signs a decree commuting the death sentences of all convicts on Russia's death row.

2000
- Cote D'Ivoire and Malta abolish the death penalty for all crimes.
- Albania abolishes the death penalty for ordinary crimes.

Jan. 31, 2000
- Illinois Gov. George Ryan declares a moratorium on Illinois executions and appoints a Commission on Capital Punishment to review the administration of the death penalty and make recommendations.

December 2000
- Texas leads other U.S. states in executions by executing forty inmates that year.
- Oklahoma was runner-up at eleven executions.

2001
- Bosnia-Herzegovina abolishes the death penalty for all crimes.
- Chile abolishes the death penalty for ordinary crimes.

Jun. 11, 2001
- Timothy McVeigh, the Oklahoma City Bomber, becomes the first federal prisoner to be executed in thirty-eight years.

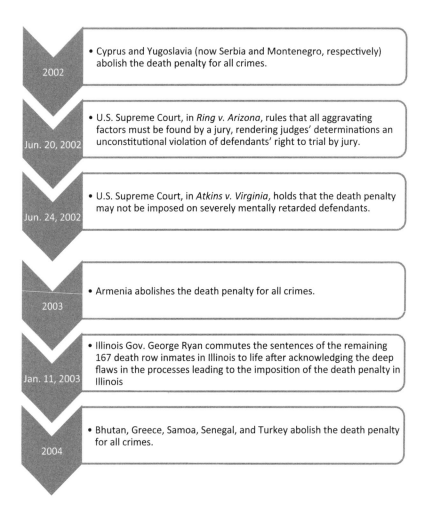

2002
- Cyprus and Yugoslavia (now Serbia and Montenegro, respectively) abolish the death penalty for all crimes.

Jun. 20, 2002
- U.S. Supreme Court, in *Ring v. Arizona*, rules that all aggravating factors must be found by a jury, rendering judges' determinations an unconstitutional violation of defendants' right to trial by jury.

Jun. 24, 2002
- U.S. Supreme Court, in *Atkins v. Virginia*, holds that the death penalty may not be imposed on severely mentally retarded defendants.

2003
- Armenia abolishes the death penalty for all crimes.

Jan. 11, 2003
- Illinois Gov. George Ryan commutes the sentences of the remaining 167 death row inmates in Illinois to life after acknowledging the deep flaws in the processes leading to the imposition of the death penalty in Illinois

2004
- Bhutan, Greece, Samoa, Senegal, and Turkey abolish the death penalty for all crimes.

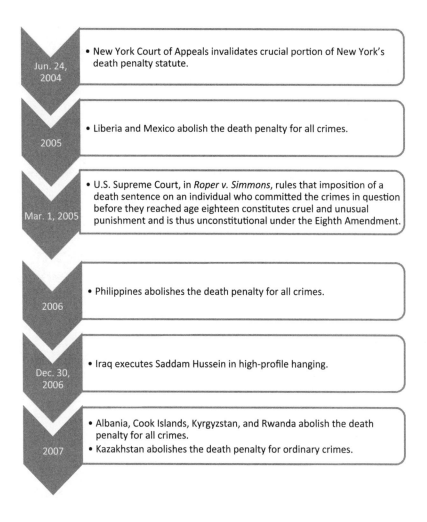

Jun. 24, 2004

- New York Court of Appeals invalidates crucial portion of New York's death penalty statute.

2005

- Liberia and Mexico abolish the death penalty for all crimes.

Mar. 1, 2005

- U.S. Supreme Court, in *Roper v. Simmons*, rules that imposition of a death sentence on an individual who committed the crimes in question before they reached age eighteen constitutes cruel and unusual punishment and is thus unconstitutional under the Eighth Amendment.

2006

- Philippines abolishes the death penalty for all crimes.

Dec. 30, 2006

- Iraq executes Saddam Hussein in high-profile hanging.

2007

- Albania, Cook Islands, Kyrgyzstan, and Rwanda abolish the death penalty for all crimes.
- Kazakhstan abolishes the death penalty for ordinary crimes.

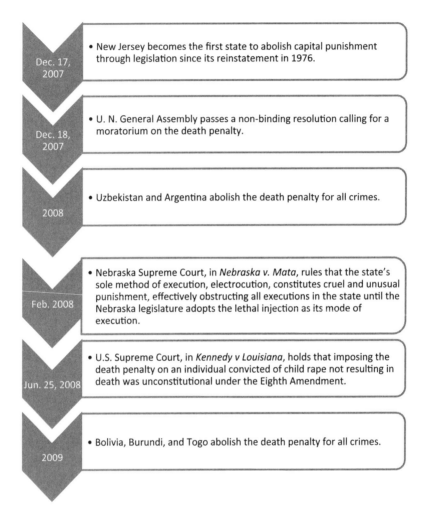

Dec. 17, 2007
• New Jersey becomes the first state to abolish capital punishment through legislation since its reinstatement in 1976.

Dec. 18, 2007
• U. N. General Assembly passes a non-binding resolution calling for a moratorium on the death penalty.

2008
• Uzbekistan and Argentina abolish the death penalty for all crimes.

Feb. 2008
• Nebraska Supreme Court, in *Nebraska v. Mata*, rules that the state's sole method of execution, electrocution, constitutes cruel and unusual punishment, effectively obstructing all executions in the state until the Nebraska legislature adopts the lethal injection as its mode of execution.

Jun. 25, 2008
• U.S. Supreme Court, in *Kennedy v Louisiana*, holds that imposing the death penalty on an individual convicted of child rape not resulting in death was unconstitutional under the Eighth Amendment.

2009
• Bolivia, Burundi, and Togo abolish the death penalty for all crimes.

Mar. 18, 2009
- New Mexico Gov. Bill Richardson signs legislation repealing the death penalty in New Mexico and replacing it with life without parole.

Sept. 30, 2009
- Texas Gov. Rick Perry removes Chairman and two other members of the Texas Forensic Science Commission just as the commission was set to hear from an arson expert who would have cast doubt on the guilt of Cameron T. Willingham, who was executed for murder by arson.

Dec. 8, 2009
- Ohio performs first execution using a one-drug lethal injection.

Jan. - Dec. 2009
- United States hands down the lowest annual number of death sentences since the death penalty was reinstated in 1976.

2010
- Gabon abolishes the death penalty for all crimes.

Jan. 18, 2010
- Ronnie Lee Gardner, convicted for murder in Utah, becomes the first person to be executed by firing squad in fourteen years and, subsequently, the last individual executed by firing squad to date.

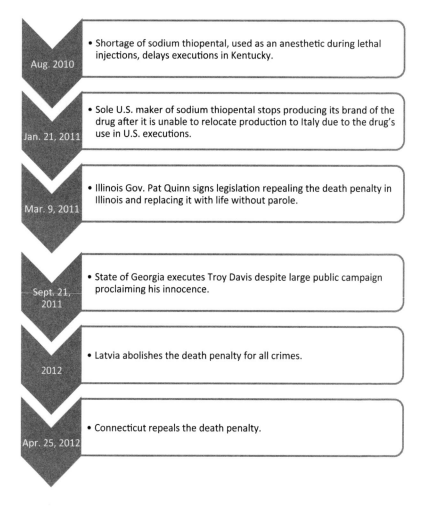

Aug. 2010
- Shortage of sodium thiopental, used as an anesthetic during lethal injections, delays executions in Kentucky.

Jan. 21, 2011
- Sole U.S. maker of sodium thiopental stops producing its brand of the drug after it is unable to relocate production to Italy due to the drug's use in U.S. executions.

Mar. 9, 2011
- Illinois Gov. Pat Quinn signs legislation repealing the death penalty in Illinois and replacing it with life without parole.

Sept. 21, 2011
- State of Georgia executes Troy Davis despite large public campaign proclaiming his innocence.

2012
- Latvia abolishes the death penalty for all crimes.

Apr. 25, 2012
- Connecticut repeals the death penalty.

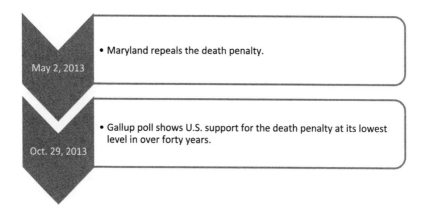

May 2, 2013
- Maryland repeals the death penalty.

Oct. 29, 2013
- Gallup poll shows U.S. support for the death penalty at its lowest level in over forty years.

APPENDIX B: COUNTRIES WITH AND WITHOUT THE DEATH PENALTY

Map and tables courtesy of the Death Penalty Information Center: http://www.deathpenaltyinfo.org/abolitionist-and-retentionist-countries.

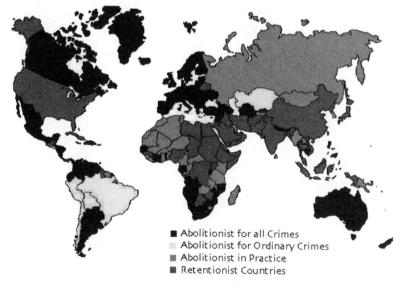

■ Abolitionist for all Crimes
▨ Abolitionist for Ordinary Crimes
▨ Abolitionist in Practice
■ Retentionist Countries

Abolitionist and Retentionist Countries Map

Abolitionist for All Crimes*

Albania	Andorra	Angola
Argentina	Armenia	Australia
Austria	Azerbaijan	Belgium
Bhutan	Bolivia	Bosnia-Herzegovina
Bulgaria	Burundi	Cambodia
Canada	Cape Verde	Colombia
Cook Islands	Costa Rica	Cote d'Ivoire
Croatia	Cyprus	Czech Republic
Denmark	Djibouti	Dominican Republic
Ecuador	Estonia	Finland
France	Gabon	Georgia
Germany	Greece	Guinea-Bissau
Haiti	Holy See	Honduras
Hungary	Iceland	Ireland
Italy	Kiribati	Kyrgyzstan
Latvia	Liechtenstein	Lithuania
Luxembourg	Macedonia (former Yugoslav Republic)	Malta
Marshall Islands	Mauritius	Mexico
Micronesia (Federated States)	Moldova	Monaco
Montenegro	Mozambique	Namibia
Nepal	Netherlands	New Zealand
Nicaragua	Niue	Norway
Palau	Panama	Paraguay
Philippines	Poland	Portugal
Romania	Rwanda	Samoa
San Marino	São Tomé and Principe	Senegal
Serbia	Seychelles	Slovakia
Slovenia	Solomon Islands	South Africa
Spain	Sweden	Switzerland
Timor-Leste	Togo	Turkey
Turkmenistan	Tuvalu	Ukraine

| United Kingdom | Uruguay | Uzbekistan |
| Vanuatu | Venezuela | |

°Countries whose laws do not provide for the death penalty for any crime.

Abolitionist for "Ordinary Crimes" Only*

Brazil	Chile	El Salvador
Fiji	Israel	Kazakhstan
Peru		

°Countries whose laws provide for the death penalty only for exceptional crimes such as crimes under military law or crimes committed in exceptional circumstances.

Abolitionist in Practice*

Algeria	Benin	Brunei Darussalam
Burkina Faso	Cameroon	Central African Republic
Congo (Republic)	Eritrea	Ghana
Grenada	Kenya	Korea (South)
Laos	Liberia	Madagascar
Malawi	Maldives	Mali
Mauritania	Mongolia	Morocco
Myanmar	Nauru	Niger
Papua New Guinea	Russian Federation	Sierra Leone
Sri Lanka	Suriname	Swaziland
Tajikistan	Tanzania	Tonga
Tunisia	Zambia	

°Countries that retain the death penalty for ordinary crimes such as murder but can be considered abolitionist in practice in that they have not executed anyone during the past ten years and are believed to have a policy or established practice of not carrying out executions. The list also includes countries that have made an international commitment not to use the death penalty.

Retentionist Countries*

Afghanistan	Antigua and Barbuda	Bahamas
Bahrain	Bangladesh	Barbados
Belarus	Belize	Botswana
Chad	China	Comoros
Congo (Democratic Republic)	Cuba	Dominica
Egypt	Equatorial Guinea	Ethiopia

Gambia	Guatemala	Guinea
Guyana	India	Indonesia
Iran	Iraq	Jamaica
Japan	Jordan	Korea (North)
Kuwait	Lebanon	Lesotho
Libya	Malaysia	Nigeria
Oman	Pakistan	Palestinian Authority
Qatar	Saint Kitts & Nevis	Saint Lucia
Saint Vincent & Grenadines	Saudi Arabia	Singapore
Somalia	South Sudan	Sudan
Syria	Taiwan	Thailand
Trinidad and Tobago	Uganda	United Arab Emirates
United States of America	Vietnam	Yemen
Zimbabwe		

°Countries that retain the death penalty for ordinary crimes.

Countries That Have Abolished the Death Penalty since 1976

1976   PORTUGAL abolished the death penalty for all crimes.

1978   DENMARK abolished the death penalty for all crimes.

1979   LUXEMBOURG, NICARAGUA, and NORWAY abolished the death penalty for all crimes. BRAZIL, FIJI, and PERU abolished the death penalty for ordinary crimes.

1981   FRANCE and CAPE VERDE abolished the death penalty for all crimes.

1982   The NETHERLANDS abolished the death penalty for all crimes.

1983   CYPRUS and EL SALVADOR abolished the death penalty for ordinary crimes.

1984   ARGENTINA abolished the death penalty for ordinary crimes.

1985   AUSTRALIA abolished the death penalty for all crimes.

1987   HAITI, LIECHTENSTEIN, and the GERMAN DEMOCRATIC REPUBLIC[1] abolished the death penalty for all crimes.

1989   CAMBODIA, NEW ZEALAND, ROMANIA, and SLOVENIA[2] abolished the death penalty for all crimes.

1990   ANDORRA, CROATIA, the CZECH AND SLOVAK FEDERAL REPUBLIC,[3] HUNGARY, IRELAND, MOZAMBIQUE, NAMIBIA, and SÃO TOMÉ AND PRINCIPE abolished the death penalty for all crimes.

1992   ANGOLA, PARAGUAY, and SWITZERLAND abolished the death penalty for all crimes.

1993	GUINEA-BISSAU, HONG KONG,[4] and SEYCHELLES abolished the death penalty for all crimes. GREECE abolished the death penalty for ordinary crimes.
1994	ITALY abolished the death penalty for all crimes.
1995	DJIBOUTI, MAURITIUS, MOLDOVA, and SPAIN abolished the death penalty for all crimes.
1996	BELGIUM abolished the death penalty for all crimes.
1997	GEORGIA, NEPAL, POLAND, and SOUTH AFRICA abolished the death penalty for all crimes. BOLIVIA and BOSNIA-HERZEGOVINA abolished the death penalty for ordinary crimes.
1998	AZERBAIJAN, BULGARIA, CANADA, ESTONIA, LITHUANIA, and the UNITED KINGDOM abolished the death penalty for all crimes.
1999	EAST TIMOR, TURKMENISTAN, and UKRAINE abolished the death penalty for all crimes. LATVIA[5] abolished the death penalty for ordinary crimes.
2000	COTE D'IVOIRE and MALTA abolished the death penalty for all crimes. ALBANIA[6] abolished the death penalty for ordinary crimes.
2001	BOSNIA-HERZEGOVINA[7] abolished the death penalty for all crimes. CHILE abolished the death penalty for ordinary crimes.
2002	TURKEY abolished the death penalty for ordinary crimes. The FEDERAL REPUBLIC OF YUGOSLAVIA (now two states SERBIA and MONTENEGRO),[8] and CYPRUS abolished the death penalty for all crimes.
2003	ARMENIA abolished the death penalty for ordinary crimes.
2004	BHUTAN, SAMOA, SENEGAL, and TURKEY abolished the death penalty for all crimes.
2005	LIBERIA[9] and MEXICO abolished the death penalty for all crimes.
2006	PHILIPPINES abolished the death penalty for all crimes.
2007	ALBANIA and RWANDA abolished the death penalty for all crimes. KYRGYZSTAN abolished the death penalty for ordinary crimes.
2008	UZBEKISTAN, CHILE, and ARGENTINA abolished the death penalty for all crimes.
2009	BURUNDI and TOGO abolished the death penalty for all crimes.
2010	GABON removed the death penalty from its legislation.
2012	LATVIA abolished the death penalty for all crimes.

2013   BOLIVIA abolished the death penalty for all crimes.

1. In 1990 the German Democratic Republic became unified with the Federal Republic of Germany, where the death penalty had been abolished in 1949.
2. Slovenia and Croatia abolished the death penalty while they were still republics of the Socialist Federal Republic of Yugoslavia. The two republics became independent in 1991.
3. In 1993 the Czech and Slovak Federal Republic divided into two states, the Czech Republic and Slovakia.
4. In 1997 Hong Kong was returned to Chinese rule as a special administrative region of China. Amnesty International understands that Hong Kong will remain abolitionist.
5. In 1999 the Latvian parliament voted to ratify Protocol No. 6 to the European Convention on Human Rights, abolishing the death penalty for peacetime offenses.
6. In 2007 Albania ratified Protocol No. 13 to the European Convention on Human Rights, abolishing the death penalty in all circumstances. In 2000 it had ratified Protocol No. 6 to the European Convention on Human Rights, abolishing the death penalty for peacetime offenses.
7. In 2001 Bosnia-Herzegovina ratified the Second Optional Protocol to the International Covenant on Civil and Political Rights, abolishing the death penalty for all crimes.
8. Montenegro had already abolished the death penalty in 2002 when it was part of a state union with Serbia. It became an independent member state of the United Nations on 28 June 2006. Its ratification of Protocol No. 13 to the European Convention on Human Rights, abolishing the death penalty in all circumstances, came into effect on 6 June 2006.
9. In 2005 Liberia ratified the Second Optional Protocol to the International Covenant on Civil and Political Rights, abolishing the death penalty for all crimes.

APPENDIX C: STATES WITH AND WITHOUT THE DEATH PENALTY

Tables courtesy of the Death Penalty Information Center: http://www.deathpenaltyinfo.org/abolitionist-and-retentionist-countries.

States with the Death Penalty (32)

Alabama	Arizona	Arkansas	California	Colorado
Delaware	Florida	Georgia	Idaho	Indiana
Kansas	Kentucky	Louisiana	Mississippi	Missouri
Montana	Nebraska	Nevada	New Hampshire	North Carolina
Ohio	Oklahoma	Oregon	Pennsylvania	South Carolina
South Dakota	Tennessee	Texas	Utah	Virginia
Washington	Wyoming	U.S. Government	U.S. Military	

States without the Death Penalty (18) (year abolished in parentheses)

Alaska (1957)	Connecticut* (2012)	Hawaii (1957)
Illinois (2011)	Iowa (1965)	Maine (1887)
Maryland† (2013)	Massachusetts (1984)	Michigan (1846)
Minnesota (1911)	New Jersey (2007)	New Mexico‡ (2009)

New York (2007)§   North Dakota (1973)   Rhode Island (1984)**

Vermont (1964)   West Virginia (1965)   Wisconsin (1853)

Dist. of Columbia (1981)

°In April 2012, Connecticut voted to abolish the death penalty. However, the repeal was not retroactive, leaving eleven people on the state's death row.

†In May, 2013, Maryland abolished the death penalty. However, the repeal was not retroactive, leaving five people on the state's death row.

‡In March 2009, New Mexico voted to abolish the death penalty. However, the repeal was not retroactive, leaving two people on the state's death row.

§In 2004, the New York Court of Appeals held that a portion of the state's death penalty law was unconstitutional. In 2007, they ruled that their prior holding applied to the last remaining person on the state's death row. The legislature has voted down attempts to restore the statute.

°°In 1979, the Supreme Court of Rhode Island held that a statute making a death sentence mandatory for someone who killed a fellow prisoner was unconstitutional. The legislature removed the statute in 1984.

NOTES

PREFACE

1. http://deathpenaltyinfo.org/node/5760.

2. During that period, 8,776 people were executed and 276 of those executions went wrong in some way. Of all the methods used, lethal injection had the highest rate of botched executions—about 7 percent.

1. THE DEATH PENALTY YESTERDAY AND TODAY

1. *Gary Gilmore: A Fight to Die* (A&E Television Networks, 1998).

2. *Furman v. Georgia*, 408 U.S. 238 (1972).

3. *Gregg v. Georgia*, 428 U.S. 153 (1976).

4. DPIC, "Part 1: History of the Death Penalty," Death Penalty Information Center, 2014, http://www.deathpenaltyinfo.org/part-i-history-death-penalty (last visited February 13, 2014).

5. Matthew 26:63–66 (KJV).

6. National Humanities Center, Toolbox Library: Primary Resources in U.S. History and Literature, "First Arrivals," in *American Beginnings: 1492–1690*, http://nationalhumanitiescen ter.org/pds/amerbegin/settlement/text1/text1read.htm (last visited February 13, 2014).

7. DPIC, *supra* note iv.

8. Michel Foucault, *Discipline and Punish: The Birth of the Prison*, trans. Alan Sheriden (New York: Vintage, 1977).

9. William S. McFeely, *Trial and Error: Capital Punishment in U.S. History*, History Matters, http://historymatters.gmu.edu/d/ 5420 (last visited February 14, 2014).

10. DPIC, *supra* note iv.

11. *Trop v. Dulles*, 356 U.S. 86 (1958).

12. *United States v. Jackson*, 390 U.S. 570 (1968).

13. *Witherspoon v. Illinois*, 391 U.S. 510 (1968).

14. *Furman*, 408 U.S. at 313 (J. White, concurring).

15. *Id.* at 365 (J. Marshall, concurring).

16. For a fascinating look at the personalities and politics behind this decision and the ones that follow in 1976, take a look at Evan J. Mandery's *A Wild Justice: The Death and Resurrection of Capital Punishment in America* (New York: W. W. Norton, 2013).

17. *Woodson v. North Carolina*, 428 U.S. 280 (1976).

18. *Gregg*, 428 U.S. at 164–66.

19. *Id.* at 195.

20. Florida used to allow judge override prior to 2002; a capital jury's sentencing decision in Indiana was merely a recommendation that the trial court was not required to follow. The 2002 General Assembly amended the death penalty statute to provide that if a jury unanimously reaches a recommendation, the trial court must "sentence accordingly." IC 35-50-2-9.

21. See Mark Costanzo and Lawrence T. White, "An Overview of the Death Penalty and Capital Trials: History, Current Status,

Legal Procedures, and Cost," *Journal of Social Issues* 50, no. 2 (1994).

22. James S. Liebman et al., *Capital Attrition: Error Rates in Capital Cases, 1973–1995*, 78 Tex. L. Rev. 1839, 1847 (2000).

23. *Id.* at 1849.

24. *Id.* at 1850.

25. For example, in one case in Georgia, Mrs. Machetti, who was the mastermind, had her conviction overturned, had a new trial, and has received a life sentence because in the county where her trial was held women were unconstitutionally underrepresented in the jury pool. *Machetti v. Linahan*, 679 F.2d 236 (11th Cir. 1982). Her lawyers timely raised this constitutional objection. They won; she lives. Unfortunately her codefendant, John Eldon Smith, tried in the same county by a jury drawn from the same unconstitutionally composed jury pool, does not. Because his lawyers did not timely raise the unconstitutionality of the jury pool, the courts ruled he couldn't raise it and he was executed by electrocution on December 15, 1983. *Smith v. Kemp*, 715 F.2d 1459, 1476 (11th Cir. 1983) (J. Hatchett, concurring in part and dissenting in part). http://www.deathpenaltyinfo.org/john-smith.

26. DPIC, "The Innocence List," Death Penalty Information Center, last updated October 25, 2013, http://www.deathpenaltyinfo.org/innocence-list-those-freed-death-row#exonerate.

27. See Alexander Volokh, "Better That Ten Guilty Men . . . ," in *Beyond a Reasonable Doubt* (Larry King, ed., 2006), available at http://works.bepress.com/cgi/viewcontent.cgi?article=1016& context=alexander_volokh.

28. *Antiterrorism and Effective Death Penalty Act of 1996*, Pub. L. No. 104–132, § 105, 110 Stat. 1214 (codified as amended at 28 U.S.C. § 2255 (2006)).

29. *Id.* § 103 (codified as amended at Fed R. App. P. 22 (1996)).

30. *Id.* § 104 (codified as amended at 28 U.S.C. § 2254 (2006)).

31. *Id.* § 106 (codified as amended at 28 U.S.C. § 2244 (2006)).

32. See John Blume et al., "The Gutting of Habeas for State Defendants," *National Law Journal* (2011) (describing the injustice of closing the doors to federal habeas corpus relief to defendants who may have lacked appointed post-conviction counsel in states that do not provide them) (excerpts available at http://standdown.typepad.com/weblog/2011/05/national-law-journal-commentary-on-habeas.html).

33. See National Research Council, "Deterrence and the Death Penalty," Report Brief 1–2 (2012), prepared by the Committee on Law and Justice (describing the consistent lack of correlation between the death penalty and homicide deterrence).

34. http://www.chicagotribune.com/news/politics/chi-chicagodays-greylord-story,0,4025843.story

35. See *The High Cost of the Death Penalty*, Death Penalty Focus (last visited February 19, 2014), http://www.deathpenalty.org/article.php?id=42.

36. "America's Retreat from the Death Penalty," *New York Times* (January 1, 2013), http://www.nytimes.com/2013/01/02/opinion/americas-retreat-from-the-death-penalty.html.

37. See "Abolitionist and Retentionist Countries," Death Penalty Information Center, December 31, 2012, http://www.deathpenaltyinfo.org/abolitionist-and-retentionist-countries.

2. MORAL AND RELIGIOUS UNDERPINNINGS OF THE DEATH PENALTY

1. When Paul, the head officer on death row, visits John's attorney to inquire whether he thought John, who was by all appearances a kind and caring individual, really committed the crimes that sent him to death row, the lawyer analogizes the seeming aberration to when his dog, who had never bitten a soul, mauled his son, telling Paul: ". . . my dog never bit before, but I didn't concern myself with that. I went out with my rifle, grabbed his collar, and blew his brains out." *The Green Mile*, directed by Frank Darabont, based on the novel by Stephen King, performance by Gary Sinise (Warner Bros., 1999), accessed January 31, 2014.

2. The White House, in the past ten years, has supported seeking death, either through capital punishment or drone strikes and tactical missions, for several individuals they perceive as serious threats to the United States, including Osama Bin Laden, Khalid Sheikh Mohammed, Abd al-Rahim al-Nashiri, and Dzhokhar Tsarnaev. Moreover, in 1996, Congress passed legislation, the Antiterrorism and Effective Death Penalty Act, which limits a federal judge's ability to give capital offenders any relief in order to expedite the government's ability to carry out death sentences.

3. http://www.deathpenaltyinfo.org/costs-death-penalty.

4. Leviticus 24:19–20.

5. Genesis 19:1–29.

6. Exodus 20:13.

7. For example, the Southern Baptist Convention resolution "On Capital Punishment" (Orlando, FL: 2000).

8. "The Republican Debate at the Reagan Library," *New York Times* (September 7, 2011), accessed on December 13, 2013, at

http://www.nytimes.com/2011/09/08/us/politics/08republican-debate-text.html.

9. *Witherspoon v. Illinois*, 391 U.S. 510 (1968).

10. *Morgan v. Illinois*, 504 U.S. 719 (1992).

11. James S. Liebman, "The Overproduction of Death," *Columbia Law Review* 100, no. 8 (December 2000): 2030, 2127.

12. Alliance for Justice, "Letter to the Honorable Merrick B. Garland," *In re Complaint of Judicial Misconduct*, No. 05-13-90099, June 13, 2013, accessed on February 22, 2014, at http://www.afj.org/wp-content/uploads/2013/09/edith_jones_letter.pdf.

13. Ibid.

14. Ibid.

15. The many other officers who participated in this behavior have yet to be prosecuted or otherwise held accountable. See Matthew Walberg and William Lee, "Burge Found Guilty," *Chicago Tribune* (June 28, 2010), accessed on March 12, 2014, at http://articles.chicagotribune.com/2010-06-28/news/ct-met-burge-trial-0629-20100628_1_burge-chicago-police-cmdr-special-cook-county-prosecutors.

16. DPIC, "Innocence and the Death Penalty," Death Penalty Information Center, 2014, accessed on February 1, 2014, at http://www.deathpenaltyinfo.org/innocence-and-death-penalty.

17. Jerry Givens, "I Was Virginia's Executioner from 1982 to 1999. Any Questions for Me?" Series: A Day's Work, *Guardian* (November 21, 2013), accessed on January 15, 2014, at http://www.theguardian.com/commentisfree/2013/nov/21/death-penalty-former-executioner-jerry-givens.

3. THE MEDIA AS A MESSENGER
OF DEATH

1. I have drawn liberally in this chapter from a previous article, "Criminal Coverage: News, Media, Legal Commentary, and
the Crucible of the Presumption of Innocence," *Reynolds Courts
and Media Law Journal* 1 (2011): 427.

2. William Nelson, *Documents Relating to the Colonial History of the State of New Jersey* (New Jersey Published Archives,
1917), First Series, Vol. 29, pp. 32–33. Digital book accessed on
March 27, 2014, at http://books.google.com/books?id=
p00OAAAAIAAJ&printsec=frontcover#v=twopage&q&f=false.

3. Charles Rowan, "Trial by Tabloid," *Marquette Law Review*
16, no. 3 (April 1932): 208.

4. Richard Rubin, "The Ghosts of Emmett Till," *New York
Times* (July 31, 2005), NYTimes.com, accessed on March 30,
2014, at http://www.nytimes.com/2005/07/31/magazine/31TILL.
html.

5. Christopher S. Kudlac, *Public Executions: The Death Penalty and the Media* (Praeger: 2007), 27.

6. Ibid., 19.

7. Craig Haney, "Media Criminology and the Death Penalty,"
DePaul Law Review 58 (2009): 689, 693.

8. Christo Lassiter, "TV or Not TV—That Is the Question,"
Journal of Criminal Law and Criminology 86 (1996): 928, 930.

9. Ibid.

10. Haney, "Media Criminology and the Death Penalty," 694.

11. Lisa A. Kort-Butler and Kelley J. Sittner Hartshorn,
"Watching the Detectives: Crime Programming, Fear of Crime,
and Attitudes about the Criminal Justice System," *Sociological
Quarterly* 52, no. 1 (Winter 2011): 36–55.

12. Ibid., 39.

13. See, for example, Anthony McCartney, "Lohan Begins Serving Sentence on House Arrest," ABC News, May 26, 2011, available at http://abcnews.go.com/Entertainment/wireStory?id= 13694427

14. See, for example, Alan Duke, "Trial of Michael Jackson's Doctor Delayed until September," CNN, May 2, 2011, http://www.cnn.com/2011/CRIME/05/02/conrad.murray.trial/index. html.

15. See, for example, Lizette Alvarez, "A Murder Trial as Tourist Draw in Central Florida," *New York Times*, June 25, 2011, available at http://www.nytimes.com/2011/06/26/us/26casey.html.

16. See, for example, "Nancy Grace Exclusive Interview with Susan Smith's Ex-husband," CNN, http://nancygrace.blogs.cnn. com/2010/08/19/nancy-grace-exclusive-interview-with-susan-smiths-ex-husband.

17. See Nancy Grace, "Essential Guide to the Casey Anthony Trial," CNN, http://nancygrace.blogs.cnn.com/category/casey-anthony.

18. Radio Television Digital News Association, *Cameras in the Court: A State-by-State Guide*, produced by Kathy Kirby and Kat Scott of Wiley Rein LLP, June 13, 2014, http://www.rtdna.org/pages/media_items/cameras-in-the-court-a-state-by-state-guide55.php.

19. State judges run for election in most states, including Florida and Illinois. See John Schwartz, "Effort Begun to End Voting for Judges," *New York Times*, http://www.nytimes.com/2009/12/24/us/24judges.html.

20. See, for example, Nancy Grace removing a lawyer from her show who disagreed with her approach to coverage of a specific case. "Nancy Grace Kicks KTRS' McGraw Milhaven Off Show," YouTube, http://www.youtube.com/watch?v=2luB5kwSymA. (Nancy Grace says, "You're off. Cut his mic.")

21. See, for example, Jessica Hopper, "Casey Anthony's Lawyer Jose Baez Has Trials of His Own," ABC News, http://abcnews.go.com/US/casey-anthony-trial-defense-attorney-jose-baez/story?id=13784113 (last visited July 17, 2011).

22. Ibid. See also Nathan Koppel, "Jose Baez: From High School Dropout to Lawyer/Celebrity," *Wall Street Journal Law Blog*, July 12, 2011, http://blogs.wsj.com/law/2011/07/12/jose-baez-from-high-school-dropout-to-lawyercelebrity/?mod=google_news_blog (last visited July 17, 2011). It certainly has been my experience and that of many others whenever we have been involved in a high-profile case that we get attacked in this way. In fact this happens even when the case is not high profile. As a death penalty defense attorney, I have been treated as though I committed the murder that my client is charged with.

23. Note 1, *supra.*

24. I have drawn here from another article of mine, "Mixed Media: Popular Culture and Race and Their Effect on Jury Selection," *DePaul Law Review* 58 (2009): 861.

25. R. Lance Holbert et al., "Fear, Authority, and Justice: Crime-Related TV Viewing and Endorsements of Capital Punishment and Gun Ownership," *Journalism and Mass Communication Quarterly* 81, no. 2 (2004): 343; Susan Bandes, "Fear Factor: The Role in Media in Covering and Shaping the Death Penalty," *Ohio State Journal of Criminal Law* 1 (2004): 585; Adeno Addis, "Recycling in Hell," Symposium: Criminal Law, Criminal Justice and Race Essay, *Tulane Law Review* 67 (June 1993): 2253.

26. Bandes, "Fear Factor," 585, 587.

27. Connie McNeely, "Perceptions of the Criminal Justice System: Television Imagery and Public Knowledge in the United States," *Journal of Criminal Justice and Popular Culture* 1 (1995): 3–5, 10.

28. David A. Harris, "The Appearance of Justice: Court TV, Conventional Television, and Public Understanding of the Criminal Justice System," *Arizona Law Review* 35 (1993): 785, 809.

29. Paul Colomy et al., "Making Youth Violence Visible: The News Media and the Summer of Violence," *Denver University Law Review* 77 (2000): 661, 672–673.

30. Ibid.; Aya Gruber, "Victim Wrongs: The Case for a General Criminal Defense Based on Wrongful Victim Behavior in an Era of Victims' Rights," *Temple Law Review* 76 (2003): 645.

31. Some of this section is drawn from other writings by the author. See Andrea D. Lyon, "But He Doesn't *Look* Retarded: Challenges to Jury Selection in the Capital Case for the Mentally Retarded Client Not Excluded under *Atkins v. Virginia*," upcoming in the *DePaul Law Review* symposium issue, 2007; Andrea D. Lyon et al., *Illinois Capital Defense Motions Manual* (2d ed. 2005); Andrea D. Lyon, "Defending the Death Penalty Case: What Makes Death Different?" *Mercer Law Review* 42 (1991): 695; Andrea D. Lyon, "Defending the Life-or-Death Case," *American Bar Association Litigation Journal* 32, no. 2 (Winter 2006): 45.

32. 391 U.S. 510 (1968).

33. 448 U.S. 38 (1980).

34. 469 U.S. 412 (1984).

35. Compare *Witherspoon v. Illinois*, 391 U.S. 510, 520 n. 9, 522 n. 21 (1968) with *Adams v. Texas*, 448 U.S. 38, 45 (1980) ("*prevent or substantially impair* the performance of his duties as a juror . . .") and *Wainwright v. Witt*, 469 U.S. 412 (1985) at 424 ("standard is whether the juror's views would '*prevent or substantially impair* the performance of his duties as a juror . . .'").

36. See *Morgan v. Illinois*, 504 U.S. 719 (1992) (venire must be questioned regarding pro–capital punishment, potentially disqualifying views).

37. "Presumably, under today's decision a juror who thinks a 'bad childhood' is never mitigating must also be excluded." *Id.* at 744 (J. Scalia, dissenting).

38. See Craig Haney, "On the Selection of Capital Juries: The Biasing Effects of the Death Qualification Process," *Law and Human Behavior* 8 (1984): 121; Craig Haney, "Examining Death Qualification: Further Analysis of the Process Effect," *Law and Human Behavior* 8 (1984): 133.

39. *Morgan,* 727; U.S. Constitution, Amendment XIV.

40. *Morgan,* 729.

41. Dr. Sunwolf, *Practical Jury Dynamics: From One Juror's Trial Perceptions to the Group's Decision-Making Process* (Lexis Nexis Group: 2004), p. 119; Richard K. Gabriel, "Values, Beliefs, and Demographics in Selecting Jurors," *ATLA-CLE* (Winter 2002): 49.

42. Gabriel, "Values, Beliefs, and Demographics in Selecting Jurors"; Ray Surette, "The Media, the Public, and Criminal Justice Policy," *Journal of the Institute of Justice and International Studies* 39 (2003): 43.

43. Sara Sun Beale, "The News Media's Influence on Criminal Justice Policy: How Market-Driven News Promotes Punitiveness," *William and Mary Law Review* 48 (2006): 397, 459.

44. Sarah Eschholz, "Crime on Televison: Issues in Criminal Justice," *Journal of the Institute of Justice and International Studies* 9 (2003): 9–11.

45. Kimberlianne Podlas, "As Seen on TV: The Normative Influence of Syndi-Court on Contemporary American Litigiousness," *Villanova Sports and Entertainment Law Journal* 11, no. 1 (2004): 19–23.

46. Ken Armstrong and Steve Mills, "Part I: Death Row Justice Derailed," *Chicago Tribune*, November 14, 1999, accessed March 30, 2014, at http://articles.chicagotribune.com/1999-11-14/news/

chi-991114deathillinois1_1_capital-punishment-death-row-
criminal-justice-system.

47. George Ryan, "Governor Ryan Declares Moratorium on
Executions, Will Appoint Commission to Review Capital Punishment System," *Illinois Government News Network*, January 31,
2000, accessed January 21, 2014, at http://www3.illinois.gov/
PressReleases/showpressrelease.cfm?subjectid=3&recnum=359.

48. Jodi Wilgoren, "Citing Issue of Fairness, Governor Clears
Out Death Row in Illinois," *New York Times*, January 12, 2003,
accessed on February 5, 2013, at http://www.nytimes.com/2003/
01/12/us/citing-issue-of-fairness-governor-clears-out-death-row-
in-illinois.html.

49. Christopher Wills, "Illinois Gov. Pat Quinn Abolishes
Death Penalty, Clears Death Row," *Washington Post*, March 9,
2011, accessed on March 1, 2014, at http://www.washingtonpost.
com/wp-dyn/content/article/2011/03/09/AR2011030900319.html.

4. THE DEATH PENALTY AS
A POLITICAL TOOL

1. Andrea Lyon, "Defending the Life-or-Death Case,"
American Bar Association Litigation Journal 32, no. 2 (Winter
2006).

2. *Keeney v. Tamayo-Reyes*, 504 U.S. 1 (1992).

3. 28 U.S.C. sec. 2254(e)(2)(A).

4. 571 U.S. ____ (2013), cert. denied November 13, 2013.

5. *Id.* at page 2 of slip opinion.

6. *Id.* at page 7 of slip opinion.

7. J. Marceau and H. Whitson, "The Cost of Colorado's Death
Penalty," *University of Denver Criminal Law Review* 3 (2013):
145.

8. 373 U.S. 83 (1963).

9. See, for example, the Michael Morton case from Texas, "Ex-Prosecutor Gets 10 Days in Jail over Michael Morton Case," *Dallas Morning News*, November 8, 2013, http://www.dallasnews. com/news/local-news/20131108-ex-prosecutor-gets-10-days-in-jail-over-michael-morton-case.ece.

10. Peter Joy and Kevin C. McMunigal, "Contingent Rewards for Prosecutors?" *Criminal Justice Magazine* 26, no. 3 (Fall 2011), accessed on March 1, 2014, at http://www.americanbar.org/ content/dam/aba/publications/criminal_justice_magazine/fall_ Ethics.authcheckdam.pdf.

11. "Prosecutors Suspended for Not Charging Man Who Burned Family after Previous Threat," January 15, 2013, CBS News, accessed on March 2, 2014, at http://chicago.cbslocal.com/ 2013/01/15/prosecutors-suspended-for-not-charging-man-who-burned-family-after-previous-threat.

12. Mitch Dudek, "Prosecutor Says She Quit after Demotion for Dropping Charges in 'Wilding' Case," *Chicago Sun-Times*, August 6, 2013, accessed on March 2, 2014, at http://www.suntimes. com/21770721-761/ex-prosecutor-i-was-demoted-for-dropping-charges-in-wilding.html.

13. *Witherspoon v. Illinois*, 391 U.S. 510 (1968).

14. *Batson v. Kentucky*, 476 U.S. 79 (1986).

15. Melynda J. Price, "Performing Discretion or Performing Discrimination: Race, Ritual, and Peremptory Challenges in Capital Jury Selection," *Michigan Journal of Race and Law* 15 (2009): 57.

16. For a more in-depth analysis about the effect of the death-qualification process on jurors, see John H. Blume et al., "Probing 'Life Qualification' Through Expanded Voir Dire," *Hofstra Law Review* 29 (2001): 1209, 1232.

17. Adam M. Clark, "An Investigation of Death Qualification as a Violation of the Rights of Jurors," *Buffalo Public Interest Law Journal* 24 (2006): 8.

18. Ibid.

19. Alyssa Newcomb and John Schriffen, "Jodi Arias Jurors: 'She Is Sentenced to Death No Matter What,'" *Good Morning America*, reprinted in ABC News, May 26, 2013, accessed on December 20, 2013, at http://abcnews.go.com/US/jodi-arias-jurors-sentenced-death-matter/story?id=19259867.

20. Kyle Hightower, "Jeff Ashton, Prosecutor in Casey Anthony Case, Runs for State Attorney Seat," *Huffington Post Miami*, August 8, 2012, accessed on March 16, 2014, at http://www.huffingtonpost.com/2012/08/08/jeff-ashton-casey-anthony-prosecution-state-attorney-campaign_n_1756782.html.

21. *American Experience: People & Events: Lynching in America,* "The Murder of Emmett Till," PBS (2009), accessed on March 12, 2014, at http://www.pbs.org/wgbh/amex/till/peopleevents/e_lynch.html.

22. See *Furman v. Georgia*, 408 U.S. 238 (1972).

23. *Id.* at 251.

24. *Id.* at 309–10 (J. Stewart, concurring).

25. *McCleskey v. Kemp*, 481 U.S. 279 (1987).

26. Kathy Lohr, "FBI Re-Examines 1946 Lynching Case," NPR, July 25, 2006, accessed on January 14, 2014, at http://www.npr.org/templates/story/story.php?storyId=5579862.

27. DPIC, "National Statistics on the Death Penalty and Race," Death Penalty Information Center, February 26, 2014, accessed on February 1, 2014, at http://www.deathpenaltyinfo.org/race-death-row-inmates-executed-1976?scid=5&did=184#racestat.

28. Richard C. Dieter, "The Death Penalty in Black and White: Who Lives, Who Dies, Who Decides," Death Penalty Information Center, June 1998, accessed on March 3, 2014, at http://www.

deathpenaltyinfo.org/death-penalty-black-and-white-who-lives-who-dies-who-decides.

29. For an example of the types of cases that get capital murder prosecutions, see Paresh Dave, "Gang Member Sentenced to Death for Four Murders in East L.A.," January 17, 2014, accessed on March 11, 2014, at http://articles.latimes.com/2014/jan/17/local/la-me-ln-gang-member-death-sentence-20140117; see also Jack Leonard, "Gang Member Sentenced to Death for 49th Street Massacre Called 'Evil,'" *Los Angeles Times*, September 6, 2013, accessed on March 11, 2014, at http://articles.latimes.com/2013/sep/06/local/la-me-ln-49th-street-massacre-20130906.

30. To read the judge's order, visit https://www.aclu.org/files/assets/rja_order_12-13-12.pdf.

31. Judge's order, 15–17.

32. The "cheat-sheet" can be found here: https://www.aclu.org/files/assets/batson_justifications_da_cheat_sheet.pdf.

33. David R. Dow, "Death Penalty, Still Racist and Arbitrary," *New York Times*, July 8, 2011, accessed on March 12, 2014, at http://www.nytimes.com/2011/07/09/opinion/09dow.html.

34. *Abu-Jamal v. Horn et al.*, 520 F.3d 272 (2008).

35. Ian Millhiser, "The Ugly Campaign to Punish a Civil Rights Lawyer Because He Helped Save a Man from Execution," *Think Progress*, February 10, 2014, accessed on March 15, 2014, at http://thinkprogress.org/justice/2014/02/10/3268871/nauseating-campaign-punish-civil-rights-lawyer-helped-save-man-execution/.

36. Peter Roff, "A Vote Against Law and Order," *U.S. News & World Report: Opinion*, March 12, 2014, accessed on March 13, 2014, at http://www.usnews.com/opinion/blogs/peter-roff/2014/03/12/democrats-who-voted-for-debo-adegbile-could-see-trouble-in-2014.

5. THE FAILURE AND FATE OF CAPITAL PUNISHMENT

1. John Conroy, "This Is a Magic Can," *Chicago Reader*, May 25, 2000, accessed on April 1, 2014, at http://www.chicagoreader.com/chicago/this-is-a-magic-can/Content?oid=902363.

2. *People v. Hobley*, 182 Ill. 2d 404 (1998).

3. *People v. Hobley*, 159 Ill. 2d 272, 202 Ill. Dec. 256, 637 N.E.2d 992 (1994).

4. That dismissal was unanimously reversed in May 1998 and remanded for discovery and an evidentiary hearing on certain *Brady* issues and a juror interference issue, in *People v. Hobley*, 182 Ill. 2d 404, 231 Ill. Dec. 321, 696 N.E.2d 313 (1998). Judge Dennis Porter (who was not the trial judge, but has been the judge on all post-conviction proceedings) presided over the evidentiary hearing over the course of the last two years. On July 8, 2002, Judge Porter denied petitioner any relief. Petitioner filed a Notice of Appeal of Judge Porter's ruling to the Illinois Supreme Court on July 10, 2002.

5. ITRC, "Mission and Procedures Statement," Illinois Torture and Inquiry Relief Commission (2013), accessed on April 1, 2014, at https://www2.illinois.gov/itrc/Pages/default.aspx.

6. As the Illinois Supreme Court stated, "After some difficulties, Stewart stated that defendant 'favored' the man who purchased the gasoline. He also stated that he could not tell with 'any degree of certainty.' At trial, Stewart expressed more certainty, but acknowledged that he saw the man's face for only three to four seconds." *People v. Hobley*, 182 Ill. 2d at 413.

7. Jodi Wilgoren, "4 Death Row Inmates Are Pardoned," *New York Times*, January 11, 2013, accessed on March 1, 2014, at http://www.nytimes.com/2003/01/11/us/4-death-row-inmates-are-pardoned.html.

8. See *Lockhart v. McCree*, 476 U.S. 162 (1986).

INDEX

ABOUT THE AUTHOR

Professor **Andrea D. Lyon** is the dean of Valparaiso University School of Law. Before taking that position, she was the associate dean for clinical programs, director of the Center for Justice in Capital Cases, and clinical professor of law at DePaul University College of Law. Professor Lyon graduated from Rutgers University and from the Antioch School of Law. She first worked for the Cook County Public Defender's Office in the felony trial division, post-conviction/habeas corpus unit, preliminary hearing/first municipal (misdemeanor) unit, and the appeals division. Her last position there was as chief of the Homicide Task Force, a twenty-two-lawyer unit representing persons accused of homicides. She has tried more than 130 homicide cases, both while in the public defender's office and since leaving that office. In 1990 she founded the Illinois Capital Resource Center and served as its director until joining the University of Michigan Law School faculty as an assistant clinical professor in 1995.

A winner of the prestigious National Legal Aid and Defender Association's Reginald Heber Smith Award for best advocate for the poor in the country, Professor Lyon is a nationally recognized expert in the field of death penalty defense and a frequent continuing legal education teacher throughout the country. In 1998, she was awarded the "Justice for All" Award at the National Conference on Wrongful Convictions and the Death Penalty. In 2003, she received the lifetime achievement award from the Illinois Association of Criminal Defense Lawyers. In 2011 she received the Outstanding Legal Service Award from the National Coalition to Abolish the Death Penalty. She has defended more than thirty potential capital cases at the trial level and has taken nineteen through the death penalty phase—winning all nineteen. She is the author of *Angel of Death Row: My Life as a Death Penalty Defense Lawyer* (Kaplan, 2010). Read more at http://andrealyon.com.